Kingdom Publishers

Let the Healer In
Copyright © Helen Aigbe – Joseph

All rights reserved. No part of this book may be
reproduced in any form by photocopying
or any electronic or mechanical means,
including information storage or retrieve systems,
without permission in writing from both
the copyright owner and the publisher of the book.
The right of Helen Aigbe – Joseph to be identified
as the author of this work has been asserted by her
in accordance with the Copyright, Designs
and Patents Act 1988 and any subsequent
amendments thereto. A catalogue record
for this book is available from the British Library.

All scripture quotations have been taken
from the New King James Version.
(Copyright © 1982 by Thomas Nelson, Inc.)
New International Version®,
(Copyright © 1973, 1978, 1984
International Bible Society) and KJV.

ISBN: 978-1-913247-03-4

1st Edition by Kingdom Publishers
Kingdom Publishers
London, UK

DEDICATION

This book is dedicated to the many who are expecting the glorious hope of overcoming grief and loss, in particular widows and widowers, in memory of Mr. Price E. Dafiaghor, my loving brother.

ACKNOWLEDGEMENT

I am truly grateful to my husband and friend, Reverend Kingsley Aigbe-Joseph, whose outstanding support is beyond comprehension.

I also thank our daughters—Stephanie, Salome, and Daisy—the Father's priceless gifts to us. Your support and prayers have made this book possible.

Thank you to Rose Efih, my amazing sister whose unconditional love has helped me and continues to do so. To Jummy, my personal intercessor and to Pastor Gideon Reuben and the Britwell Baptist Church for their prayers and support.

Special thanks go to Vanessa, my niece, for her contribution and to our wonderful mother, Mrs. Susannah Dafiaghor for her ceaseless prayers.

I thank Blessing, Nonto, Magnus, and Lynette for showing me firsthand how the Lord transforms His saints from one degree of glory to another.

I also thank Patti and Jackie; mamas close to my heart.

I appreciate greatly my publisher, editor, and their staff, and of course, everyone whose lives have touched me and the ministry to widows and the bereaved.

My heartfelt thanks go to Helga Taylor and to Reverends Janice McVeigh-Flores and Gerry Flores for endorsing this book.

Thank you also to Teresa Davies, my prayer partner, with whom I have shared and grown.

Father, with my every gratitude, I thank You for giving me the privilege of carrying something of Your heart and the honour of sharing it by Your Spirit with Your saints and the many who You will to read this book.

ENDORSEMENT

It was my honour to be asked and has been my privilege to write the Endorsement to this book, a book for our time. It highlights the importance of the ministry to widows possibly forgotten by some Christians and churches, just as it was forgotten in the early Church, as written about in the Book of Acts (see Acts 6:1-6).

This book is innovative and biblically challenging. I particularly admire Helen's depth of scriptural understanding and her application of the Scriptures to the practical ministry and care of widows. It has a deeply empathic approach, incorporating known patterns of grieving, the mourning process, and person-centred pastoral skills. Helen encourages the "carer" to offer a safe and supportive relationship through good listening skills while recognising the limits of such a role and encouraging appropriate referral if that would be helpful.

There are many valuable, useful and practical suggestions to carers and widows alike. I particularly resonate with her meditative approach and suggestions. The spiritual dimension undergirds every page, while her understanding of how mourning and grieving may affect our prayer life and walk with God, brings the reader a sense of peace.

Helen points the widow towards hope and offers a way through the process of mourning and grief. This book is a modern-day challenge to churches, pastors, and deacons. It begs us to ask ourselves the questions: "How are our widows being cared for in our church today, and is the Lord pleased with us?"

I commend this book to you.

Helga Talor
ACCREDITED COUNSELLOR, TRAINER,
SUPERVISOR AND COUNSELLOR MANAGER
UNITED CHURCHES OF HEALING MINISTRIES
HUDDERSFIELD, UNITED KINGDOM

I highly recommend this book to you. It is well written and stirs us to not just speak about it, but demonstrate the Love of the Lord and the importance of caring for one another.

A few years ago, both of us suffered great pain, grief and loss when we suddenly and unexpectedly, became widow and widower when our late spouses went home to Glory after unfortunately, both experienced cancer.

However, that was not the end but rather a brand new beginning. God, in His infinite grace and mercy, brought us together, and we fell in love, got married and are about to celebrate our first Wedding Anniversary, this month!

We have just begun to step out in Ministry again, and although it is still the same Vision; that of a '5-fold equipping' Ministry especially focussed on the Apostolic and Prophetic, the Lord gave us a new name and instructed us just to demonstrate His Love to a lost and hurting people!

We re-named our Ministry: XTREME LOVE!

Through our experiences though, the greatest thing we had to endure was loneliness. It was excruciating. However, as we both allowed God to come and gradually heal our hearts, we were able to move on.

God wants to take us beyond the place we find ourselves in and move us on, into His eternal Plans and purposes for our lives, so we can fulfil our ultimate destiny. But we do need to "Let go and Let God".

In the words of a Worship song we sing entitled: I Could Sing of Your Love Forever:

Over the mountains and the sea, Your River runs with love for me, And I will open up my heart, and let the Healer set me free.

It's about opening up our broken hearts and letting God heal us. The more we are healed, the more we can release healing to others.

Isaiah 61.v.1-3:

1: The Spirit of the Sovereign Lord is on me,

because the Lord has anointed me, to proclaim good news to the poor. He has sent me to bind up the broken hearted, to proclaim freedom for the captives and release from darkness for the prisoners.

2: to proclaim the year of the Lord's favour and the day of vengeance of our God, to comfort all who mourn,

3: and provide for those who grieve in Zion, to bestow on them a crown of beauty, instead of ashes, the oil of joy instead of mourning and a garment of praise, instead of a spirit of despair.

This book says it all really.

Rev. Janice McVeigh-Flores and Gerry Flores
XTREME LOVE

CONTENTS

Rise up and come Away

Men in Grief

The Broken Hearted

Through the Eyes of a Teenager

Grief and Mourning

Loss of Identity and Grief

Hope and Redemption

A Special Group in the House

It's a Family Affair

The Unsung Army

At The City Gate

The Hurting Mother

Shedding the Past

Conclusion

All Bible quotes are from the New King James Bible (©1982 Thomas Nelson) unless otherwise specified

PREFACE

This is a book of hope, consolation, and most of all, overcoming pain, hurt, and bereavement. It looks at the different types of bereavement we face and the changes that come with the transitions from our winter season to our springtime. Also this book covers the varied aspects of loss, and there are a number of chapters dedicated to care and support for the widows in the Body of Christ.

There is a group in the Body of Christ that needs some degree of care and recognition in the church besides the orphans. Whether it is secular counselling, psychotherapy, pastoral counselling, or Christian counselling of any kind for bereavement, separation, or any sort of loss, I believe the group most in need of it is the widows. I hope you agree.

I have carried a burden to plead the cause of widows in the church for almost ten years. As a result, the plea in this book is not aimed at professionals who have learned the art or skills of care, but at individuals, the Church, Christian organisations, and even those outside of church whose desire it is to give comfort through listening, visiting, and practical help to the bereaved and the hurting.

This book is also aimed at anyone dealing with and overcoming depression, grief and loss of identity. It deals with grief and worship, shedding the past, and coming into your new season. It is a book of God's comfort in times of bereavement, family hardship, difficult marriages, divorce, job and loss of income, loss of relationships or friendships, and church splits through betrayal and other loss of any kind.

There is a lost art of care in the Body of Christ as it was practiced in the early church (see Acts 6:1-7) This is one of the three commandments given to the Gentile churches by the apostle James and the elders in Jerusalem.

In this book, there is a brief look at the definition of grief and mourning and the place of mourning. I offer suggested ways the bereaved can overcome bereavement. We shall also look at some suggested ways a family member, a friend, or a neighbour can help the bereaved and ways a local church or Christian organization can provide the much-needed support framework that a widow or a hurting person needs. We avoid blanket service and instead target the individual needs of a widow or the hurting.

This book is a voice-driven vehicle with the aim that it will serve as a tool to re-awaken the Body of Christ to our responsibility first to the silent community—the widows in the Body of Christ—and then beyond. It is also a book that offers support to anybody who is reaching for the glorious hope of overcoming the pain of loss and grief of any kind.

This is by no means a counselling tool, but a book that encourages you to visit the widows and the orphans and anyone who is hurting in their time of affliction, for that is pure religion indeed. (See James 1:27.)

Chapter ONE

Rise Up and Come Away

> *The voice of my beloved! Behold, he comes leaping upon the mountains, skipping upon the hills. My beloved is like a gazelle or a young stag. Behold, he stands behind our wall; he is looking through the windows, gazing through the lattice. My beloved spoke, and said to me: "Rise up, my love, my fair one, and come away. For lo, the winter is past, the rain is over and gone. The flowers appear on the earth; the time of singing has come, and the voice of the turtledove is heard in our land. The fig tree puts forth her green figs, and the vines with the tender grapes give a good smell. Rise up, my love, my fair one, and come away!"*
> (Song of Solomon 2:8-13)

I lay in the hospital bed and a lady leaned over me with a gentle whisper in my ear.

"We can't get your baby to breathe," she said.

At first, I could not comprehend what she said as I concentrated on the doctor working furiously to stitch me up following an episiotomy.

"We can't get your baby to breathe," she said again. And then it dawned on me that my baby was stillborn. As the shock of the news spread through the room, Dele, my birth partner, sat speechless, and my sister, Rose, was crying out, "No Lord! No Lord!"

This cannot be happening, I thought. I remembered the doctor handing my baby to me before handing her to the paediatrician, and she felt heavy in my hands. Little did I know that I was holding a stillborn baby girl. I turned to the paediatrician and said, "Work on her," in a tone that said, "*You must be joking.*" I asked my sister, who had been with me while I was in labour, to immediately call our local church to pray. I was sure that because it was Easter, the resurrection power of the Lord would raise my baby.

It was Easter Sunday, April 11, 1993. Such was my faith in the Lord to raise my baby. After all, I thought, *God will not give and then take away.* Besides, I had carried this pregnancy alone as my husband was stuck in Nigeria as he lacked the immigration status to join me in the United Kingdom. Oh yes, I had more than one reason why the Lord should raise Ruth (my husband named her before she was born)

But He did not!

As the hours rolled into days and then into weeks before the burial, I lost the appetite for living and begged the Lord every night not to wake me up the next morning, knowing that He has power to kill and make alive (see 1 Sam. 2:6) Strangely, I woke up every morning with a song that said, "Lord You are so good and I love You so...because You are so good to me."

Gradually, with no husband by my side to comfort me, I began to hear the voice of the Lover of my Soul who was standing behind the wall, gazing through the windows of my soul, saying: My fair one, rise up and come away with Me, because this night season and the winter is temporary.

The Scripture from Song of Solomon 2 came alive to me as I began a very slow process of recovery that lasted eight long years; even though my husband was able to join me and we went on to have two beautiful girls during that time.

Throughout my journey of recovery, every step I took reminded me that in order to embrace my seasons of spring and summer, there had to be a total coming away from the winter season before I could enjoy the new season. Although I had two beautiful girls and was now settled in the United Kingdom with my husband, I could not get past the pain of losing Ruth without shedding tears.

Slowly, I learned that even though there is a transition between the midnight and dawn, it is natural to hang on to the midnight season when the dawn is already here. Exhaustion or staying up late can cause you to sleep a little longer, but someone would come and wake you up saying, "It's morning." That was how the voice of my Beloved spoke and beckoned me to rise up, because my winter was now past.

This is a call to go past the pain and sufferings of our fallen world, rising above every circumstance, however bitter or painful, hearing the voice of the One who loves our souls, and embracing the comfort His voice brings.

More than Recovery

When we look around us, we see and experience the loss of loved ones, divorce through families breaking up due to unfaithfulness, alcohol abuse, pornography, and loss of homes or finances due to job loss, to mention but a few. We see children who have left home for wild living like the prodigal son in Luke 15 and even churches are splitting due to betrayals, misunderstandings, church politics, and sometimes even greed. These are some of the things that lead to pain and loss and to a place of grief and mourning.

God created us as relational beings; first with Him and then with one another. We can only do well when our relationship with Him takes top priority. As I heeded His voice to rise up and come away from my winter season, I gently learned that trees can 'clap their hands' as the leaves rustle together in the gentle breeze, that the smell of the earth after the rain and the scent of the flowers were sweet fragrances, if I stopped to breathe deeply. These revelations gave me a new sense of thankfulness. I heard the chirping and singing of birds in the early hours of the mornings as the sun is peeping through the clouds. I even stop now to observe the moon every night and watch its various shapes take form and I am in awe of the wonders of God.

Now my heart sings with the psalmist:

The heavens declare the glory of the God; and the firmament shows His handiwork. Day unto day utters speech and night unto night reveals knowledge. (Psalm. 19:1-2)

The death of our daughter, Ruth, was compounded by the fact that my husband was absent, although unintentionally, at the time I needed him most. As I directed my disappointment at him, I knew I was blaming God for all this mishap. But the thought had settled in my heart that I must be paying for some earlier sin. Otherwise, how could I explain this tragedy?

Nevertheless, in the midst of this grief, I learned that when God trusts you with tragedy, He is seeking to enlarge your soul - the seat of your will, intellect and emotions. Tragedies do not come from Him, but He uses them to work out His ultimate purpose for our lives. I further learned that He was not only calling me out to be with Him and enjoy an open relationship with Him, but His desire for me was to come into intimacy with Him, which speaks of oneness with Him.

The more I yielded to Him; my soul began to open up. Just the whisper of His name filled my soul, and as I entered more and more into worship, my lips began to sing in my sleep.

...moving gently the lips of sleepers. (Song of Solomon 7:9)

I learned that sometimes the greatest worship is just whispering His name, and the soothing and calming effect it brings, is priceless.

Your name is ointment poured forth. (Song of Solomon 1:3)

Worship becomes the attitude of the heart when the heart, not just the knees, bows before God. This experience of intimacy has now positioned me to describe Him to others through personal experience, having heard His voice, felt His touch, and gazed on Him. As mothers often kiss their children's pain or hurt better, in this place of intimacy, my grief and mourning were not only kissed better, but were kissed away.

Let him kiss me with the kisses of his mouth — for your love is better than wine. (Song of Solomon 1:2)

In the same way, God wants to awaken your heart to love, adoration and the ability to truly worship, for the Father seeks those who will worship Him in spirit and in truth.

Every pain, hurt, grief and loss launched at you, becomes a tool in the hands of God to draw you in as a true Worshipper, and, the fact that God is seeking them, means that true Worshippers are few and far between.

The Psalm of David becomes an experience you can share:

I will bless the Lord who has given me counsel; my heart also instructs me in the night seasons. (Ps. 16:7)

You will learn the ability to climb over your night seasons — the seasons of fear, dread, pain, bereavement, mourning, grief and loss — and come out on the other side a more wholesome person. As they say of our everyday products, a more "improved" version. You become a stable and a balanced person who, like a knight who stayed on his horse and holds firm with the stirrups, can fight and overcome without falling.

PRAYER

Heavenly Father, God of all comfort, open my heart and pour out Your warmth to heal the ache and pain in my heart. As I open my heart, may the sweet fragrance of Jesus' Name fill my heart and mind to come forth and may I experience the sunshine Your love gives, in Jesus Name.

Chapter TWO

Men In Grief

ELIJAH

We shall begin by looking at the life of Elijah. In 1 Kings 18, Elijah had scored a huge victory over Baal and its prophets and killed over four hundred Baal 'prophets' as he (Elijah) called down fire from Heaven to demonstrate that God is the one true God who alone deserves our worship. At what seemed to be the height of Elijah's ministry, a single threat from a woman sent him running for his life, leading him to a huge downhill slide. We are not told in Scripture whether Elijah saw this attack coming or not, but it is obvious that he was totally unprepared for it.

When my husband and I suffered a huge backlash following a very successful prayer meeting, I fell into months of depression. I remember saying to the Lord that I was no use to my husband, our young children or even the ministry.

Then a look at Elijah's life brought me hope. We can read about God and hear about God and hardly be affected, but when we feel His presence or hear His voice, it takes us to whole new level of hope. Every question, anger or rage directed at the Lord only drew Him nearer to me and brought me to a place where I could hear from Him as to my next place and assignment. For example, Elijah despaired to the point that He prayed to die, but God knew that his assignment was not yet done, and so He twice sent an angel to feed him.

But he himself went a day's journey into the wilderness, and came and sat down under a juniper tree: and he requested for himself that he might die; and said, It is enough; now, O Lord, take away my life; for I am not better than my fathers. (1 Kings 19:4 KJV)

We often forget or circumvent the place of praise when we are in the place of depression or feeling suicidal like Elijah. Elijah left his servant in Beersheba of Judah — meaning praise — and proceeded to go to the wilderness, to a desert with no food, water or people. I know from experience and from many others that we not only lose our appetites by choice or design, we tend to also avoid people in our times of depression.

I believe that depression is tougher on men than on women because women tend to talk to others, making the depression a problem shared, while men do not. Maybe that is why the suicide rate is higher with men than with women.

But the antidote to depression is praise, for the Joy of the Lord is our strength. (see Nehemiah. 8:10) It is in praising Him that we rise above our circumstances.

God slowly brought Elijah via a long journey of forty days, to the place where he (Elijah) could have a divine encounter with Him (God) and then return with renewed vigour to finish his assignment.

So too, the Lord works with each of His children who are in deep depression, to bring them back to a place of hope and strength. This divine encounter with the individual in such a deep state of depression moves one from knowing the Bible and revelation of Christ as just a message of truth, to reaching a place of realising it as a personal message of Love. This realisation of His love for us forces us to remember that He is in the boat of our turbulence all the while, and therefore, we will not be overwhelmed or go under.

Just like the disciples' experience, do we wonder if the Lord has gone to sleep when we need Him most? He was fast asleep in the same boat with the disciples when a furious storm arose without warning (see Matt. 8:23-27) This sounds like a situation you or somebody you know might be familiar with or even in right now — a sudden loss of a loved one, a marriage or a job. The Lord will immediately respond when we call on Him, for there is always divine intervention at the most turbulent times of our lives.

The Losses Suffered by Job

Whatever the reason that has led an individual into a place of despair — whether it be death of a loved one, divorce, loss of friendship or even the loss of a congregation through betrayal or church politics — there is always a divine visitation from God in your night or winter season.

Job lost his children and everything he owned; making him curse the day he was born. He had friends who spoke out of turn for God and only served to aggravate his pain, yet the time came when he turned his attention to God and God answered him out of the whirlwind. This divine encounter made Job reply to the Lord:

> *I have heard of You by the hearing of the ear, but now my eye sees You. Therefore I abhor myself, and repent in dust and ashes.* (Job 42:5-6)

Until we get affected by His voice or presence, we are full of vanity and pride. Like Elijah, we think we are the only ones zealous for the Lord, until He tells us that there are seven thousand more prophets who equally love the Lord and have not bowed their knees to other gods.

When we are favoured by a divine visit, it is a joy to be treasured; but the strength we derive from such an encounter changes our perspective of Him forever. We no longer ask questions like, "Why me, Lord?" We simply say, "Your Kingdom come. Your will be done on earth as it is in heaven" (Matt. 6:10)

Quite often, we forget that our Lord Jesus — our great High Priest who has passed through the heavens, the Son of God — can sympathise with our weaknesses because He was tempted as we are, although He remained without sin. (see Hebrew. 4:14-15)

The Lord Jesus suffered separation through the loss of His followers, and in one day, a group of seventy was reduced to just twelve simply because He told them some truths they had not heard before about the requirements and perils of following Him.

The Betrayal of Jesus

The Lord is also well acquainted with the feelings of betrayal and rejection. He came to His own and His own did not receive Him. (see John 1)

A pastor or a leader of a ministry may be going through the hurt and pain of betrayal by a trusted friend or assistant pastor who has split off with some of the congregation. Still, he or she can draw comfort from knowing that the Lord went through the same betrayal and came out as a conqueror. Your "faithful twelve" will not only stand and build with you, but your experience will result into an explosion for His Kingdom.

A long while ago, I was struggling with a friendship that I felt justified to terminate when the Lord asked me, "What would you do with a friend whom you know is not only a thief but will eventually betray you?"

I know that, when the Lord asks me a question, it is because He is prepared to give me the answer. Simply put, the Lord said to me not to speak evil of anyone, for even His closest disciples knew nothing of this betrayal. I also know that it is not my place to terminate any relationship, but that, too, is His prerogative for my life. I learned, not just from reading His Word but from that place of prayer, that the Lord Jesus only did what the Father wanted Him to do and did not follow His own will.

The Lord knew what it meant to be betrayed and abandoned in His very hour of need by His closest friends. He even knew what it meant to be misunderstood by family members and ultimately separated from God, His Father, for three hours on the Cross through no fault of His own. The most powerful example God gives of being in the depths of despair, is Jesus in the Garden of Gethsemane; that night He became sorrowful even to the point of death, over His coming death on the Cross.

> *And He took with Him Peter and the two sons of Zebedee, and He began to be sorrowful and deeply distressed. Then He said to them, "My soul is exceedingly sorrowful, even to death. Stay here and watch with Me"* (Matthew 26:37-38)

When Jesus was confronted with depression, He responded by calling for a prayer team. When that failed, He prayed alone, earnestly, and God responded by sending an angel to strengthen Him just before He was crucified. As a result, He was strengthened enough to confront His darkest time with the ability to ask for forgiveness for us, and ask John to take care of His mother. Even a thief could be with Him in glory just by asking Him.

Jesus carried the burden of sin for the whole world. And God suffered, and is still suffering, the spiritual separation from His creations that He made in His own image and likeness. Therefore, without any shadow of doubt, He knows how to comfort you through your time of grief, mourning, loss, bereavement, divorce, abandonment — whether by parents or spouse — betrayal, backstabbing by fellow pastors and congregation members, and even the loss of friendships.

Power to Heal

God is in the business of hearing and answering our prayers when we call on Him out of pain or despondency. The psalmist knew this when he cried out to Him:

> *Out of the depths I have cried to You, O Lord; Lord, hear my voice! Let Your ears be attentive to the voice of supplications. If You, Lord, should mark iniquities, oh Lord, who could stand? But there is forgiveness with You, that You may be feared. I wait for the Lord, my soul waits, and in His Word I do hope. My soul waits for the Lord more than those who watch for the morning— yes, more than those who watch for the morning. O Israel, hope in the Lord; for with the Lord there is mercy, and with Him is abundant redemption. And He shall redeem Israel from all his iniquities* (Psalm 130 – underlining mine)

Here, the psalmist's cry is from the depths of his soul — the seat of his mind, will, intellect, and emotions — as he waits on the Lord for the redemption and restoration of his circumstance. This earnest plea is so intense that the repetition: waiting on the Lord more than the watchman waits for the morning, drives home his desperation. On the other hand, his assurance of the abundant redemption of the Lord compels him to call on others to hope in the Lord.

> *O Israel, Hope in the Lord; for with the Lord there is mercy, and with Him is abundant redemption* (Psalm 130:7)

The power of God to heal and restore is amazing if we will let Him. We call to mind the story of Naomi who endured one loss after another and thought that her situation was beyond any form of hope imaginable. Not only did she become a widow in a foreign land, but she lost her two sons as well. She took it upon herself to try to change her name from Naomi, meaning "pleasant, delightful, or lovely," to Mara, meaning, "bitter."

We often respond to bad or harsh circumstances with bitterness together with hopelessness. Often the pain and anger are directed towards God, as Naomi says:

> *...the hand of the Lord has gone out against me!* (Ruth 1:13)

In a time of loss of a dear one — or multiple losses like in Naomi's case — we do not always see the Hand of God moving on our behalf. It is hard to see beyond our bitterness and recognise God's desire to use the situation to bless us and to reach others.

I fought for a long time with the question: "Why me?" until I slowly learned that when God trusts you with tragedy, He is seeking to enlarge your soul. This does not mean that bad things come from Him, but he can and will, bring good out of the situation.

Any time we hurt or suffer pain as a result of death, separation, drug addiction or even betrayal, the challenge we face is not to think that God is responsible for our pain. We believe the lies of Satan — whom we know is now the god of this world since Adam and Eve surrendered the world over to him as a consequence of their fall — that God is against us and not for us. We have lived in this deception for so long that we forget that what Satan means for evil, God will turn around for our good.

Satan is the author of evil. Hence, James, the brother of our Lord Jesus, says, "Do not be deceived." As we respond to God's tender touch, through a friend's phone call or a knock on the door or a card through the post, however small the ray of hope, we find that God is not only able to feel with us but is also able to touch us.

This gradual move toward His tenderness will pull you into the truth and bring you closer to the Father of all light, for it is only in His Light we see light (see Psalm. 36:9) You will be able to join with the psalmist and say,

> *They looked to Him and were radiant, and their faces were not ashamed.* (Psalm 34:5)

Be encouraged, because the best is yet to come. It did for the young man, Joseph. He suffered hate and betrayal by his brothers, was sold into slavery, and was lied about and thrown into prison, bound with fetters for a crime he did not commit. Most times, we do not know why we go through certain trials. Joseph didn't know either at the time. But we know that God was working behind the scenes as the Word of the Lord tried him. (see Psalm 105:19) Joseph became lord over Pharaoh's land and the ruler of his substance, able to teach his princes and senators wisdom.

PRAYER

Heavenly Father, may Your comfort for all those who mourn, remind me of the truth that You are beside me in the same boat that is tossed by the storms of life. May this truth become a reality of Your Love for me, to carry me safely to the shores of life, in Jesus Name.

Chapter THREE
The Broken Hearted

There is a kind of loss that many women feel way too ashamed to talk about, especially Christians.

When I reflect on it, I wonder how even I could have done it; the wilful termination of a pregnancy.

I feel I have to share my story with you, however sensitive it might be.

From shame to forgiveness

About twenty-one years ago, I arrived and settled in the United Kingdom as an unmarried young lady. I fell in love with a lovely young man who loved the Lord, and we began to court. Not long after that, we contacted our parents in Nigeria, telling them of our intention to marry here in the United Kingdom while both families met out there to carry out the traditional ceremonies.

As we were waiting for the formalities to complete, I grew very impatient and persuaded my fiancé that we could go 'all the way' as our parents had carried out the initial formalities of a traditional marriage.

The result was that I became pregnant. I felt way too embarrassed to share it with anybody, not even my pastor.

I had been given the opportunity to honour God. My pastor, Wynne Lewis, had suggested that he should bless the union while we wait for the formalities to be completed. I refused this gracious gesture, and before long, I fell into discontentment with the Lord and ended up in bed with my fiancé.

Ashamed, I terminated the pregnancy without even giving my fiancé any choice in the matter. I chose the option to be put to sleep the entire time to avoid facing the memory of it. From then on, I led a life of deceit and terrible guilt. Although I repented, the nagging feeling of this deliberate sin — sin against my unborn child — stole my joy for many years. As the reality and the gravity of my actions came home to me with every passing day, I was convinced I could never live a normal life again.

But God sent a man of God called Derek Prince to preach in

my church about a year or so later, and he brought a message that set me on the path to forgive myself, be healed and recover from my guilt. I could not remember the topic of his sermon, but I knew by the end of his message that the Lord had sent him to our church for me on that day. He mentioned the sin against the helpless as the sin of abortion and his graphic explanation made me feel both worse and better at the same time.

> *The blueness of a wound cleanses away evil: so do stripes the inward parts of the belly.* (Proverbs. 20:30 KJV)

My emotional wound, which was by now infested with shame and guilt, needed deep cleaning, however excruciating the pain of the 'stripes to the inward parts' of my being would be. The sin against my own seed, and the seeds that would have come after, created such huge a loss and separation that only a deep cleaning would result in a wholesome healing. I knew that I did not need just a quick fix to this.

Several years later, the Lord gave me this Scripture to confirm what I felt. Although my journey to a sense of forgiveness had begun from the time Derek Prince came to our church many years before, I still could not stop wondering if my baby was the son, I could have had.

God Mends the Broken hearted

The broken-heartedness I felt and carried began to lift slowly as I began to read Scriptures like David's confession,

> *A broken and contrite heart—these, O God, You will not despise.* (Psalm 51:17)

This was when he had slept with Uriah's wife and then had Uriah positioned in a battle so he would be killed.

As the mending of my spirit continued, I could sing again.

With these Scriptures, I passed through my sense of guilt and the feeling of being an outcast to a place of having the walls of life rebuilt through a total and wholesome cleansing and healing. Now I no longer carry the weight of murder or wonder in regret if my baby was the son I could have had, because the Lord has delivered me from the guilt of bloodshed, and my tongue now sings aloud of His righteousness.

Deliver me from the guilt of bloodshed, O God, the God of my salvation, and my tongue shall sing aloud of Your righteousness. (Psalm 51:14)

I do not cease to stand in awe of God's plentiful mercies as I now serve in a ministry focussed on overcoming grief and helping the hurting.

Rainbow in Dark Clouds

The rainbow is a powerful image of hope, especially when seen against the backdrop of a dark, cloudy sky. Its many bright colours remind us that we will not be overwhelmed by any circumstance, however sad it may appear to be.

The rainbow is the immense curved spectrum of light which appears only when both elements of sunshine and rainfall are present. As the sunlight enters the raindrops, it breaks up into its true colours of red, yellow, blue and violet, with red being at one end of the spectrum and violet at the other. The most commonly cited and remembered sequence in English is Newton's sevenfold red, orange, yellow, green, blue, indigo, and violet.

The first mention of a rainbow in the Bible followed the account of how God wiped out the world with the flood.

The separation God felt from man, His creation, began to grow wider and wider through human wickedness and violence, until we read that God was sorry that He had made man and He was grieved at heart.

We have read accounts in the Bible of how men like Job questioned God, asking if He knew or understood pain. The grief God felt at man's wickedness in Genesis was unbelievably deep; it brought Him to only one possible resolution — destroy humanity, beasts, all creeping things, and birds from the face of the earth.

The pain of a father or a mother at the rebellion of a child can drive him or her to disown that child. The constant reaching out in love to no avail leaves the parent in a position of wanting to give up.

As always, God's plan is never one of total annihilation. God may have repented for creating man, but never for redeeming man. Hence, He reached to the rainbow around His Throne, and threw some of it across our earth to give us a promise of never again wiping out His creation with a flood. And God said:

> *"Thus I establish My covenant with you: Never again shall all flesh be cut off by the waters of the sky; never again shall there be a flood to destroy the earth." And God said: "This is the sign of the covenant which I make between Me and you...for perpetual generations: I set My rainbow in the cloud, and it shall be for the sign of the covenant between Me and the earth"* (Genesis 9:11-13)

Therefore, the rainbow is a sign given to Noah that man need never fear that the earth will be destroyed by flood. It's also very colourful and peaceful; this effect is a sign that God wants you to remember His promise of hope and a brightly coloured future amidst dark and dreary times.

The rainbow is also a sign for new beginnings.

No matter the pain, whatever the loss, you can start all over again. We can now lay hold on our future or the new season of life. Just as God's creative power started all over again with Noah and our earth, and gave a perpetual promise of hope, so we can look upon God and the passion of the Cross which reflect His glory and becomes like the colourful rainbow.

Reflecting Him

In late July 2008, my friend and prayer partner, Teresa, paid for a trip to Geneva for us so that I could recover from the sudden death of the dear saint mentioned earlier in the book. Amidst fears and confusion, the Lord broke out in the cloud with a double rainbow in the sky on the first of August. Teresa and I rejoiced to see God's sign of, "I will keep My promise", boldly written in the sky, just for the two of us. The date of 1/08/08 with the double rainbow in the sky, confirmed for us that we can be doubly sure that "God is not a man that He should lie, neither the son of man that He should repent." (Numbers 19:23) Interestingly, I saw more rainbows that year than I can remember ever seeing in my many years living in England, confirming again to me the hope and joy of a new beginning.

In the Women of Destiny Bible (NKJV, Nashville: Thomas Nelson ©1982), La Nora Van Asdall's commentary on

Isaiah 42:9 is such a huge blessing enabling me to forget the past and reach out to the new.

She writes concerning the women who gave up their mirrors in Exodus:

He made the laver of bronze and its base of bronze, from the bronze mirrors of the serving women who assembled at the door of the tabernacle of meeting. (Exodus 38:8)

"Consider this:" she writes, "The ladies who left Egypt and followed Moses into the wilderness offered up their mirrors to build the laver in the tabernacle. As an act of worship, these women gave up the right to look upon themselves for the greater purpose of looking upon God and serving Him. That which once reflected the image of a woman now reflected the fire of the sacrifice upon the altar."

She goes on to say, "Many times our own image of ourselves keeps us from our destiny of serving God and reflecting Him. If we stop gazing upon ourselves and our past, and begin to behold Him, we will be changed. ...The past, with all its pain, will lose its power; and you will be free to be all that He has destined you to be."

What a revelation this letter was to me the first time I read it, about eight years ago! Since then, I have always found it a refreshing spring of water in my thirsty, parched, and dry seasons and, in particular, during sad times. As we gaze on His loveliness and not on ourselves, our faces will shine again and reflect the colour of a rainbow even in a dark and cloudy sky. The spectrum of light appears in the sky when the sun shines onto droplets of moisture in the Earth's atmosphere.

So too does God's Word shine into our dark and sad times to create a multicoloured arc — a banner of love over us.

PRAYER

Heavenly Father, I choose to give You my broken heart for You to mend and make whole. I repent and receive forgiveness for the sins of my past. Release me from my guilty conscience Fashion and design my heart for Your purpose and my beauty to reflect Your glory, in Jesus Name.

Chapter FOUR

Through the Eyes of a Teenager

When I lost my dad, I was a fourteen-year-old teenager and our relationship had been strained. I lost my sense of security, my home and life as I knew it was no longer. I lost all feeling. It has taken me years to be able to feel, trust, love and regain a sense of stability. I was asked how I grieved and I couldn't answer the question, but the Lord guided me to poems I wrote throughout my struggle.

Putting pen to paper has always been a coping mechanism for when I was feeling overwhelmed. Not only do these poems illustrate how I was feeling at the time, they articulate the internal dialogue that was going on in my head. The most interesting thing about this is the fact that I was writing all of this, without consciously knowing what I was feeling. As I re-read these poems, I realise that, at that time, I was suffering with depression, anxiety, loneliness and despair. For these reasons, I was numb, because the emotions would have been too much for my body to handle.

Inspire Me (27/02/2008)

Inspire me to be the person I want to be

Inspire me to try and succeed

Inspire me to grow with wisdom

Inspire me to bring peace to our kingdom

Inspire me to help others

Inspire me to be the best sister to my brothers

No matter how small, I still had hope and I still had ambition. In this poem, I am literally asking the Lord for inspiration; at the same time this also infers that I didn't have any inspiration at the time.

Filled with nothing (March 2008)

My life is empty filled with nothing!

In a small flat in Streatham (chuckles)

In my room I stay

Filled with nothing but dismay

I have nothing to do

I think I have the blues

Maybe it's me,

maybe I put myself in this situation

When I see my friends they make me happy, but that's not enough

I need fulfilment within; maybe my skin is too thin

Cobwebs and bats are probably in my heart

All I want is a good place to start

To start loving and being truly happy again

Maybe I'm thinking too hard, looking for something that isn't there

This could be a good year I'll go for the ride

And let go of my pride

I'll be the person I ought to be, even if it kills me!

Am I pretending? (March 2008)

I laugh, I smile but it's all pretend

It's a cover it's a mask

Or is my misery finally at an end?

When you stand alone in the world, it feels like you're on a deserted Island

All your feelings descend

So alone, a crowd wouldn't budge my lack of content

When will the black, dreary feelings come to an end?

I laugh, I smile but it's all pretend

O how I wish he would send me to the pearly white gates

Open me up to a beauty so rare,

Or send me an angel to look on my life and start to repair

Mend the cracks, the holes the bruises, the pain

Mend the mask I fake, just like he did for La'vette from a piece of cake.

I laugh, I smile but it's all pretend

I can't sleep or eat without struggling; the two things humans need to carry on juggling

Life's ups and downs

God works in mysterious ways they say… Why is he puzzling

I laugh, I smile but it's all pretend

They say I think deep!

It's not that deep to me

Everything has a reason a purpose for being

Too many questions I have to ask, perhaps that's why I am not content or maybe got over my past.

I laugh I smile but it's all pretend

As I start to feel sorry for myself, my thoughts turn and attack me

Snap out of it!

Get a grip; you're not even worth it

People are dying and starving, do you think you deserve it?

Do you deserve people's kindness and generosity?

Which leads me to curiosity

Why are people kind and giving?

Maybe they want to see me living?

Maybe they wanted gratitude, or they wanted me to owe them

But how do you pay someone back for such a huge favour

Do you forever in your life stop the labour?

Have you done enough?

Have you paid your dues?

Have you started to misuse?

Misuse their trust, their home even their kindness

Make sure you don't, you'll be left with loneliness

I laugh `I smile but it's all pretend

`loneliness like your shadow that stalks you in the night

Until you're in the light, then - in pops up and appears with an evil grin in sight

I laugh I smile I hope it's not pretend.

At this point, I had reconnected with my friends and all we did was laugh with each other but when I was alone, I felt so much pain that I questioned my laughter.

I describe feeling bruised, miserable and asking for death, my mind seems to spiral with negative thoughts that question everything, I was in a very dark place. I no longer trusted people's kindness, as my experience in Leeds was that of manipulation and people helping me only so they could use it against me. But there is a ray of sunshine, the poem ends with hope.

My one and only love (undated 2008)

I miss you, I love you, I wish I expressed this more

when you were with me

Now you're gone I'm not sure what's going on

I'm confused in my head

In my body I can't explain

Feelings, random thoughts playing upon my brain

Wishing you was here, but happy that you're the one

Living a stress-free life, but over here we still mourn.

Till today I still reminisce

On the days of peace, joy and happiness existed

Now you're gone and I am so pissed!

I missed my chance to say goodbye

and my one chance to tell you why -

The reasons I was so stubborn and spoilt -

I was tired of sharing you, I wanted you to myself.

I miss you and I love you

I wish I expressed this when you were here

But now it's too late, it's like you disappeared

I was with the boys and the baby mentioned your name

like you were talking to him

I was angry because I didn't get that chance to connect

But I know it's my fault for not being aware

A part of me is missing, it will never be the same

Every day I feel you watching because I know you protect me

My angel my love looking at me from above

Your grave I need to visit but it's hard for me

to accept your body is lying there

I'll stop here even though not all has been said

I'm going to sleep now

I know you watch as I lay my head.

This poem summarises my feelings at my father's death that I never got the opportunity to express.

Anger (undated)

Anger is what I feel when I can't get my own way

It's what I feel when people play

With lives and ruin them

Play with guns and knives and misuse them

Don't watch me when I'm angry because if my anger turns on you, I won't be the one to blame

When you see me quiet and silent, leave me alone

perhaps you should just leave me in my zone

All I see is red

All I hear is blurred noises

I can't take no more- SNAP!

I popped, what are you going to do?

It's too late the damage has been done

Now it's time for us to dance along to the song

You're looking at me confused and wondering why I abuse

Use abusive language towards you but I warned you

When you see me silent, I'm violent so leave me alone!

For a long time, I had a very bad temper and would get into arguments with people. This started before my father's death, from when I was twelve (two years before he passed) but my temper was heightened by his death and I was always in a fight or an aggressive argument with people, young and old, male and female. I clearly had a lot of anger inside of me that I needed to get out.

Through this process of healing (grieving), I realise I had been numb, and that the numbness began the day I saw my father's motionless body. This numbness has manifested itself throughout my life in different ways over the years, and it took me giving birth to my son, for me to begin to feel again.

I always say, "I didn't just lose my father, I also lost my home". And I continued to experience this belief for fourteen years of my life. It's taken me this long to realise that, ultimately, I have no control of what is going to happen. The only things I have control over are my present choices. Throughout everything I have been through, God has protected me and provided for me. I always found a way.

I have been angry for a long time, and I've blamed everyone around me for my suffering. I blamed them for not understanding me and not showing me empathy. I wandered through my life determined, but without direction. Each time I moved and started life again, something would happen to interrupt it and take me back to square one. This was, ultimately, because I had not released and let go of my feelings of instability. I've had to accept that the only stable place lies within me, and this place is where God is.

The people that have had the most profound impact on my life thus far are the people against whom I have carried the most anger, and now I understand; it's time to let this go.

I am starting to see that God has a plan for me. I am not

quite sure how it will unfold but my experience in life so far has taught me to have faith and believe I am favoured and blessed, and everything always works out in the end.

PRAYER

Heavenly Father, God of restoration, redeem and restore to me all the years I have lost as Your purpose unfolds in my life. May I become a testimony of Your gracious Hand of goodness and mercy upon my life. Open my eyes to behold Your beauty in all that I see as I let go off all hurt and pain, in Jesus Name.

Chapter FIVE
Grief And Mourning

I have deliberately chosen to discuss this chapter in full, later in this book, in order to first portray the message of hope and then look at the reality of pain while in mourning and grief.

In order to understand bereavement, we need to make a distinction between grief and mourning. Grief is a person's intense emotional internal pain and is related to the experience of a great loss. Mourning is an external expression of one's grief, especially when mourning for someone who has died. Both affect the whole person — the spirit, soul, and body. Consequently, I believe healing needs to be a progression from the spirit to the soul and then to the body, but not necessarily in that order.

Grief and mourning are intensely personal. We refer to stages of grief, but these may not occur in an orderly progression. Depending on the circumstances of the loss, and on the grieving individual, one may experience different stages of grief, or maybe be in and out of the same emotional state several times.

I am of the opinion that one's spirit, soul, and body grieve. I believe the human body is the last recipient of the loss, hence the initial reaction of numbness. This is followed by the human soul — the seat of your emotions. This accounts for the expressions of outbursts of tears, anger, guilt, etc.

Then the human spirit may fall into the 'spirit of heaviness' if this grieving goes untreated. The human body also responds by producing side effects like loss of appetite, insomnia, palpitations, nausea and dizziness.

In my opinion, it seems the soul takes longer to recover, and a person expresses the emotions of sadness or even depression unconsciously during events such as the anniversary of the month of death or loss.

I remember that after the death of our first child, Ruth, who was stillborn, I suffered bouts of depression every April for four years and did not know why. Each time, my husband would gently remind me that it was the anniversary of Ruth's passing. At such times, I always thanked the Lord that his (my husband's) sensitivity to my moods helped me, not only to process my emotions, but also to overcome those sad times.

However, how grief affects our spirit is difficult to articulate but a pervading sense of heaviness, nagging at the core of your being, tells you that grief is present in your spirit. This is why the scripture calls it the 'spirit of heaviness'. We also know from scripture that the antidote to this 'heaviness' is the 'garment of praise'.

When one's spirit grieves, you feel bruised on the inside, otherwise known as the "spirit of heaviness" (Isaiah 61:3) The antidote to this 'heaviness' is found in the following scripture:

> *...To comfort all who mourn, to console all who mourn in Zion, to give them beauty ... the garment of Praise for the spirit of heaviness.* (Isaiah 61:2 & 3)

As we transfer our grief onto Him (God), the divine exchange on the Cross-becomes a reality in our own lives.

These are all normal and understandable reactions to bereavement and a natural part of the mourning and grieving process. Given time, support and understanding, these reactions will lessen and eventually disappear.

But there is an even better and more excellent way — responding to the Good News of Salvation by faith as the Lord declares:

> *The Spirit of the Lord God is upon Me, because the Lord has anointed Me to preach good tidings to the poor; He has sent Me to heal the broken hearted, to proclaim liberty to the captives, and the opening of the prison to those who are bound; to proclaim the acceptable year of the Lord, and the day of vengeance of our God; to comfort all who mourn, to console those who mourn in Zion, to give them beauty for ashes, the oil of joy for mourning, the garment of praise for the spirit of heaviness; that they may be called trees of righteousness, the planting of the Lord, that He may be glorified.* (Isaiah 61:1-3)

The Lord Jesus gives, and we receive, making this declaration valid. But we must acknowledge and declare that the poor already have had the good tidings preached to them, the broken hearted have been healed, captives liberated, prisoners released, mourners comforted and consoled, beauty has already taken place of ashes, the oil of joy has been poured out for mourning, and the garment of praise has been given for heaviness.

God is waiting for you to let Him make you into a tree of righteousness. You will be His own planting so that people will see His glory on you and put their trust in Him. That is how you bring Him glory, and He is glorified.

According to Scripture, it is all right to grieve but not as those who have no hope, especially at the death of a loved one (1 Thessalonians 4:13) Grief is a deep sorrow that not only affects your emotions but also could affect your mental state and even your physical body. There are a number of factors responsible for mourning and grief. It could range from the death of a loved one to the loss of identity, insignificant as the latter might seem.

I remember an incident about six years ago, when our family moved from London to Leeds within the United Kingdom. Our home was broken into within the first three weeks of moving. We felt our privacy had been violated, and our older two daughters mourned not only the loss of our property and sentimental things like gifts from godmothers, but also the end of innocence and the not knowing if somebody was lurking in the corners of their home after nightfall.

My close friend in London was so terribly shaken by her experience with burglary that she could not shake off the ordeal for over a year. She was not only grieving the loss of her goods, but as she puts it, "Something in me went with the stolen goods."

For lack of a better explanation, vulnerability agitates this feeling of losing a part of you. During these times of loss, for some, grief brings a loss of appetite but for others, it could be the opposite — eating to numb the pain.

However, it is essential to note that there is a place for mourning according to the Word of God. Mary and Martha were still sitting on the floor with neighbours who were mourning with them, when the Lord Jesus showed up. It is recorded that the Lord wept at Lazarus' tomb. (see John 11)

Grieving is part of the cycle of life hence it is written in Isaiah: "...He has borne our grief and carried our sorrows..." (Isaiah 53:4) This is inclusive of the redemptive work at Calvary.

At the death of my brother years ago, I wailed loudly and uncontrollably at his deathbed and at the funeral. I was not sure if that was the natural thing to do or simply what we Africans do, but I knew after searching Scriptures that it was scriptural to mourn and even grieve. The difference between this grief and the first grief at the death of my stillborn baby was that, at my brother's funeral, I wept but also then knelt at the graveside, on a wet morning, to worship the Lord, even though I did not understand the sudden death of a forty-two year old man leaving behind a wife and five children. At my brother's death, I chose to worship and not question as I had done with Ruth.

I saw my mother suddenly taken ill. She was in her late seventies and was deteriorating very quickly with no medical explanation. As I began to seek the Lord, I perceived that she had not grieved properly for her son, my late brother. I remember calling to comfort her and her saying to me, "Do not cry, because the Scripture says: in everything, give thanks."

As I later found out, my mother had told everyone who came to comfort her, the same thing each time. Unbeknown to her, she had subdued her emotional pain in an unhealthy manner and this had taken its toll on her physical body.

Mourning for the Dead

It is scriptural to mourn for the dead, and we have confirmed that there is a place for mourning. We love;

therefore, we grieve. Love is a powerful emotion and our grief is the evidence that we are capable of love.

Isaiah 61:2-4 tells us how God gives *beauty for ashes, the oil of joy for mourning, the garment of praise for the spirit of heaviness.* Our God, who made tears and tells us in Ecclesiastes 3:3-4 *that there is a time to be born, a time to die, a time to weep and mourn, and a time to laugh and dance,* brings His comfort to the bereaved. This is so that they can be

> *...trees of righteousness, the planting of the Lord that He might be glorified.* (Isaiah 61:3)

It becomes more interesting, for Isaiah says that these comforted and consoled people:

> *...Shall rebuild the old ruins, they shall raise up the former desolations, and they shall repair the ruined cities, the desolations of many generations.* (Isaiah 61:4)

Tamar, Naomi, Ruth and Anna, the prophetess, are all examples of such people as God makes trophies of grace from those who yield to His comfort and become repairers of the 'desolations of many generations'. The Book of Ruth is a beautiful example of this verse.

Grief comes with mourning, bitterness, rejection, sometimes unforgiveness, and hopelessness and in some cases, even poverty, if the breadwinner is the one who passed away. In most cases, these emotions do not arise from other people, but are created by the bereaved themselves. The danger in a situation like this is the not knowing when to move from a place of bereavement to a place of hope.

The transition from grief is not defined; therefore, I describe it as one long walk in a dark tunnel that is never-ending, but when you least expect it the light is suddenly there.

When she visited the United Kingdom years ago, my Christian friend from Uganda shared with me how, after the death of her husband, she became very angry and bitter both with her dead husband and with his relatives. Her testimony of how she was healed from HIV following the death of her husband came about when she learned to forgive her husband for passing the deadly disease on to her. She mentioned that very often widows will build a wall around themselves without realising they are keeping help and support away.

My friend now calls herself "a redeemed widow", and joyously runs a ministry for widows in Uganda. She was drawn to our ministry when she heard about us from my sister at a conference while she was staying in the United Kingdom. She was eager to meet a married woman with young children, with a real burden for widows.

I often ask myself: "Why do I have such a passion for widows, when I have no idea of what a widow goes through?" One thing is clear — I have no credentials whatsoever except that this is a passion I just cannot shift.

Some married women have found it hard to connect with my vision for this ministry because they fear that they might lose their husbands. Nevertheless, one thing that put my mind to rest was when the Lord said to me that He did not have to become a sinner in order to save humankind. He knew no sin, yet He was able to identify with sin so as to deal with sin.

In the same way, I may not know the pain a widow goes through, but I have a passion to stand alongside them through their grief and mourning.

PRAYER:

Heavenly Father, help me acknowledge grief and loss as realities of life and that, through these, You are weaving a beautiful tapestry with each stroke of pain that our fallen world presents. May I not be overwhelmed with the journey of grief, but go through it and welcome the living hope that is at the end of it, in Jesus Name.

Chapter SIX

Loss Of Identity And Grief

This may appear to be a very vague title, but you must agree that there are circumstances we face, that do leave us confused and unhappy. This is common when transition occurs in our lives, like a teenager growing into adulthood, going from being single to becoming a married person, or becoming a parent.

Many young people find their identity in, and even emulate, athletes, celebrities or rock stars. An adults' identity is inter-linked with their career, hobbies or even the neighbourhood in which they live.

Image is an unconscious need within everyone because we are made in the image of God. But when we fail to realise this, there will always be a substitution, and this is compounded with any issue of grief. If the transition from one stage to another is not smooth, this could result in a loss of identity.

Paul, in writing to the Romans, tells us how easy it is to confuse our identity with anything other than God, our Creator, if we fail to retain His knowledge and be thankful.

Because, although they knew God, they did not glorify Him as God, nor were thankful...and changed the glory of the incorruptible God into an image made like corruptible man... (Romans 1:21, 23)

But there is one transition that we think less about, and that is living in and coping with a foreign environment. I had not given this much thought until I moved to the United Kingdom, married, and settled here. Since then, I have seen how emigration, whether voluntary or not, can affect a person negatively through the loss of identity. The grief that goes with this can be crippling.

Journey to Promise

Before I explore this a little further, the story of the Israelites comes to mind quite readily. When they arrived in Egypt, under the governorship of Joseph, they knew who they were. A group of seventy easily had a sense of belonging and togetherness. They quickly multiplied and became a threat to their host culture, suffered terribly and, finally, left Egypt, lock, stock and barrel.

On their journey through the wilderness to the Promised Land, they forgot their identity as a people belonging to the God of their forefathers, Abraham, Isaac and Jacob. The Bible records that they and their fathers were shepherds.

Joseph, instructing them what to tell Pharaoh while requesting settlement in Egypt, said:

> *That you shall say, "Your servants' occupation has been with livestock from our youth even till now, both we and also our fathers," that you may dwell in the land of Goshen; for every shepherd is an abomination to the Egyptians.* (Genesis 46:34)

In the years they sojourned in Egypt, they forgot the story of their forefather, Abraham. He had left his home country at the command of God, to go and live in a foreign land that was promised to him and his descendants. When the Israelites left Egypt, they forgot who they were and yearned for the lifestyle of Egypt. They did not realise that they were indirectly grieving the loss of their identity.

As a result, they gave in to complaining and murmuring. It took a while for Israel to know again that they were not like other nations. In the days of Samuel they requested an earthly king like other nations, and God granted their request. In 70AD when they ceased to be a nation, they were scattered all over the world for many centuries, but they clung to the God of Abraham, Isaac and Jacob.

Before our eyes, God performed a modern-day miracle as Israel became a nation again in 1948. What but the knowledge that they belong to God could make a group keep their culture and lifestyle in place, even though they were scattered all around the world?

Finally, the Israelites (Jews) were reunited in their homeland again as one people with one national identity.

It becomes obvious that an individual's identity is not in a person, a degree, their status in life, their profession, the people they associate with, or any such thing. When the seasons shift, as they often do, we need to know that we have an anchor in God.

Taken into captivity in a foreign land, Daniel knew that his identity was rooted in the God of his forefathers. Therefore, when his captors changed his name to reflect their pagan gods, and made him eat of the king's food, Daniel refused to defile himself.

Daniel maintained his identity in a foreign land, honoured God by standing for who he was in the Lord, and excelled in that foreign land. He excelled through difficult circumstances and did not allow the pressures of captivity to thwart God's plan and purpose for his life.

Be strong in the Lord to resist fear and doubts of who you are in Him, and believe that God can cause you to fulfil His plan for you and through you, no matter what situation or place you find yourself in. He did it for Daniel and many others, including me. He will do it for you too.

Finding Identity

I was born in the United Kingdom when my parents came to study here, and so I have dual citizenship — British and Nigerian. I left Britain very early in life and lived my teenage years and part of my adult life in Nigeria. A time came when my siblings and I returned to Britain with the help of our maternal aunt, but I did not fit into the culture and lifestyle of my country of birth.

Although I had come to know Jesus as my Lord and Saviour as a teenager, the Scripture, "Every place on which the sole of your foot treads shall be yours," (Deuteronomy 11:24)), did not work for me. This is because I had come into my country of birth with a 'grasshopper' mentality.

For many years, I barely survived although I was in church and working. My transition from living in Nigeria to living in

Britain was very rough and miserable indeed and left me feeling lost and confused. I mourned the loss of my Nigerian culture and lifestyle and mentally lived in Nigeria even though I was physically living in Britain. I short-changed my life in every aspect in Britain.

As I struggled to come to terms with living in Britain, I found that my loss of identity was only made worse as I complained bitterly about everything British and did not see the blessings in the land. Little wonder it took me almost fifteen years before I could *inherit my land*.

Every day, as the Lord brought this message home to me, it became clear that I could enter a kingdom and not inherit it. The struggles — seeing a country like Moses did, entering and inheriting a country like Joshua and Caleb, and enjoying the fruit of the land — are processes that require an intensive effort. The effort here is not laborious, but it is a matter of knowing that your identity is in the Lord, for you are His offspring no matter where you reside.

We should all draw our identity from the simple fact that, in Him, we live and move and have our being. When we begin to shape God's divine nature into something, someone or even some place, confusion sets in over who we really are.

Our times and seasons in life change from infancy to childhood, adolescence to adulthood, being single to married, divorced or bereaved to becoming single again. Some are even forced to claim asylum and become a refugee in a foreign country due to war or famine. The one thing that will carry us through these identity changes is the knowledge that you are the beloved of God who owns Heaven and earth. He has pre-appointed your times and seasons and even the boundary you occupy at any given time.

I have friends and know many others who have claimed

asylum and are now living as refugees in Britain. They may never return to their home country again. Many, by choice, have adopted Britain and are living their lives to the fullest because they know that God is not far from each and every one of us.

Whether you are in a situation or location by choice or not, knowing that you are offspring child of God provides a safety net that helps you to adjust easily to any new season in your life without giving in to misery and regrets. When we become Christians we learn to find our identity in our Creator and in doing so, we become Christ-like. Until we set aside other images we revere, it is hard to conform to the image of Jesus, for we can only conform ourselves to what we love. This is how we overcome the grief that any loss of identity brings to us.

Worship and Grief

Worship and grief are two actions that are poles apart, or so it seems. When we feel beaten by the circumstances of life or life's issues, especially where death of a loved one is concerned, worship and grief are words that we find hard to reconcile in that situation.

What is worship?

One definition of worship is: "gazing upon God." For me, this is worship. This is further expounded in F.W. Faber's song: "My God, How Wonderful Thou Art." Do you sing songs that bring you to a breathless place where all you want is to experience worshipping God with the angels and not have to come back to planet Earth?

Yes, this is one of the songs that does that to me.

My God, how wonderful Thou art, Thy majesty, how bright;

How beautiful Thy mercy seat, In depths of burning light!

...How wonderful, how beautiful, The sight of Thee must be,

Thy endless wisdom, boundless power and awesome purity!

...Yet I may love Thee too, O Lord, Almighty as Thou art,

For Thou hast stooped to ask of me, The love of my poor heart

No earthly father loves like Thee, No mother e'er so mild

Bears and forbears as Thou has done

With me, Thy sinful child.

Father of Jesus, loves reward, What rapture will it be

Prostrate before Thy throne to lie,

And gaze, and gaze on Thee.

When grief is bound up in worship, the experience is like living in bubbles, insulated from life's traumas. Unlike substance abuse that numbs you for a brief moment, this experience carries and leaves a deposit in you that restores your soul.

We know it goes against the grain of human nature to worship God when our lives fall apart. Our first inclination is to accuse and criticise God, and ask questions, such as, "How can a good God allow so much evil to happen to us?"

If we ever come to a place of worship, this is usually long after we have accused God of not living up to His end of the bargain.

The Book of Job is a good place to look when we explore the mystery of human suffering, contrasted against the unseen realm of the spirit that goes beyond the minds of ordinary men.

The Book of Job teaches us that Satan is the author of all misery and that God, the Sovereign One, ultimately controls the extent of all happenings. Satan has been licensed as the god of this world ever since the fall of man.

Job's severe trials all happen in one day, and his immediate reaction is to worship! We note that in Job 1 the phrase, "while he was still speaking", appears three times, each time reporting a new calamity to Job.

> *Then Job arose, tore his robe, and shaved his head; and he fell to the ground and worshipped. And he said: "Naked I came from my mother's womb, and naked shall I return there. The Lord gave, and the Lord has taken away; blessed be the name of the Lord." In all this, Job did not sin nor charge God with wrong.* (Job 1:20-22)

This is quite powerful. Job did not know that Satan had asked for permission to attack his character, yet his first reaction was to worship and not one of railing accusations against God or charging God with wrong.

Job violates the psychologist's formula for the stages of mourning and grief.

As we wonder at such a reaction, one thing comes to mind, Job trusted God's goodness and His boundless mercy ---

"How beautiful Thy mercy seat in depths of burning light (love)" Job had a relationship with God that defied any calamity, however inexplicable, and continued to stand firm. "Though He slay me, yet will I trust Him" (Job 13:15) He had acquainted himself with the nature and character of God. He trusted that the relationship he had with God would carry him through these severe trials. Ultimately, God has a plan of refinement in mind to conform us to the image of His dear Son, Jesus.

But He knows the way that I take; when He has tested me, I shall come forth as gold (Job 23:10)

Worshipping God in our times of grief forms music in our soul that brings us comfort in times of darkness and distress in our lives. As our souls respond, we go past the cry of, "Where is God my Maker?" to the experience that we now have a song for Him that only dark times can birth. The songs He teaches us in these times become our comfort (see Job 35:10)

As I already mentioned, when my brother suddenly passed away, I was very sure that, being a minister, the responsibility to cry out to the Lord for Him to bring my brother back to life, was mine. After all, the Lord always warned me of impending dangers — this had blind-sided me, so I was convinced that my brother would be raised. At least, that was my reasoning.

I sent everybody home in the evening, including his wife, and told the Lord that I had enough faith for Him to do His work now. Nothing happened throughout the night, and we kept him on the life-support machine for the better part of the following day with no results. I knew I had to give up my fight and went for days without much sleep or food, wondering why the Lord did not show up in my desperate situation in a foreign land. I fought the thought of how to take his corpse to an aged mother in Nigeria. I imagined what my sister-in-law must be going through with five children, including a one-year-old son. When I found no answers in my finite mind, one thing stood out for me — trust God's sovereignty and just worship.

At the graveside, amidst the tears and howling, I found a place to kneel in the wet mud. I worshipped God and said to my sister, who was beside herself with grief, "Just worship."

A few weeks later while visiting my sister-in-law, I met a family friend who said to me that many young men and their families had given their lives to the Lord Jesus Christ as a result of my brother's death. For me, this was a very comforting testimony, as it answered questions that I was uncertain about. I had dreamed about my brother before he was laid to rest. In the dream, he shared with me that he had just finished reading Judges 14-16. When I awoke from my dream, I read those Scriptures and found them to be the account of Samson.

How comforting it was to know that my brother was still in the faith, although not as active as my sister and I. Samson accomplished God's purpose for his life at his death, and I now believe that my brother fulfilled his mission too. I found the testimony of our friend, concerning my brother, very soothing.

I also witnessed the miracle of God's provision not only with the funeral, but also in provision for his wife and children.

In grief, worship becomes easy when we shift our gaze from our circumstance and look to God, prostrating ourselves before His face and gazing on Him!

PRAYER:

Heavenly Father, may this season produce a song in me and for me, so that I can help many overcome grief and they, too, will have a song for themselves and others, in Jesus Name.

Chapter **SEVEN**

Hope And Redemption

I have written quite extensively on hope for any kind of loss that an individual suffers or has suffered. However, in this chapter and those that follow, I will be focusing on emotional, practical, and spiritual support for the bereaved — especially the widow. I will be looking at ways in which an individual and also a local church can help the bereaved, and the different kinds of needs that a widow may have besides the issue of bereavement itself.

Mourning is the external expression of one's grief, and grief affects the whole of the person — the spirit, soul, and body. As a result, there will be a progression of healing from the spirit to the soul and then to the body, although not necessarily in that sequence.

I have deliberately chosen not to discuss the different stages of mourning in this book, as I believe that there are already so many books that deal with this subject. Throughout each stage — denial and isolation, anger, bargaining, depression and final acceptance of the loss — a common thread of hope emerges from one stage to another, until we finally come to a more peaceful acceptance of the death, loss or separation.

Overcoming Grief

Give yourself time to mourn. It is scriptural to mourn. A counsellor I know once said that, "Mourning is like the ebb and flow of the tide. Each time a wave beats on the shore, it does not come as far as it did the previous time."

Grief will come as a wave, but the power of grief will lessen with each subsequent beat. You get better with each day that comes along.

Allow yourself to feel emotions like anger, tears, fear, and even guilt as they come, but do not let them overcome you. God created emotions. Remember the account of my mother I mentioned earlier.

Let the Lord bear your sorrow and grief (see Isa. 53:4) Allow the Lord to carry you in this very hard time of your life. Cling to God like Ruth did to Naomi and the God of Israel.

But Ruth said: "Entreat me not to leave you, or to turn back from following after you; for wherever you go, I will go; and wherever you lodge, I will lodge; your people shall be my people, and your God, my God. Where you die, I will die, and there will I be buried. The Lord do so to me, and more also, if anything but death parts you and me (Ruth 1:16-17)

Accept comfort. Sometimes, it comes in small but significant ways, like a kind word said at the right time or even a phone call or an unannounced visit.

I remember an unannounced visit I had from a Christian friend when Ruth went to be with the Lord. Ruth was not yet buried and my husband was still in Nigeria at the time. I was hoping that my husband would be able to join me in the United Kingdom before the burial. I had made a phone call to find out from him when to expect him. I learned that the Christian friend he was living with at the time had just lost her daughter, by drowning, the day before and that my husband was the one who discovered her body.

The sudden rush of mixed emotions running through my mind began to make my head spin, and I knew that if nobody came to my rescue at the time... I fear to think what could have happened. Just then, my doorbell rang. God had sent a Christian friend to visit me in the nick of time. Oh, the amazing goodness and His wisdom when we need help most!

Moving from Grief to Hope and a Future

Here are some suggestions.

Accept God's love to combat rejection. Even though Satan will want to convince you that God is responsible for your hurt or could have prevented it. The feelings of embarrassment, humiliation, failure, or disapproval, can only be overcome through receiving and accepting God's love.

Begin to step into the place of praise. Leave anything that takes away the place of God in your life. For Ruth, it was moving from Moab, the place of idolatry, to Bethel of Judea, the house of God and the place of bread.

Start enjoying where you are going before reaching there. This requires a conscious effort to focus, and it is quite involving and intense. Allow God's Word to motivate and transform you as you put your trust in Him and His Word.

Forget the past. In a marriage relationship, you made your vows, verbally saying, "Until death do us part." The Lord may have a future of remarriage for you like He did for Ruth. You may even want to relocate like Ruth did, but you must hear the Lord. For most people it is an inner peace, and for some it is just knowing or seizing an opportunity that is right in front of them.

Every cross has to be carried by its owner, but your Sabbath rest comes with the confession of your mouth. Romans states that salvation, in other words, deliverance, comes by confession (see Romans 9:9-10) My friend from Uganda whom I mentioned earlier shared this truth with me and, of course, a few more. I may not be able to acknowledge all of them, one at a time.

Build a wall of protection by proclaiming, confessing, and overcoming the spirits of heaviness, loneliness, rejection, and hopelessness. The enemy comes in immediately when death occurs, and his main attack on the widow, among others, is the feeling that there is no more use for you. For a widow or widower whose spouse has just passed away, the low self-esteem and sense of hopelessness can set off a tidal wave of emotions that seems to be a never-ending nightmare.

The Enemy Attacks

An older friend, who is a widow from in the United States, shared this revelation with me when I was visiting America in August 2004. This was my first opportunity outside the United Kingdom to share my vision of pleading the cause of and giving recognition to widows.

She said it began in the Book of Genesis when Satan attacked the woman. He chose the area of her emotions; through her mind. But when a person, especially a widow, begins to grasp Genesis 1:11 — that change comes from the inside out and not from the outside in — then she can see things through the Word of God and not through the circumstances around her.

This can be applied to all areas of grief. The overwhelming feeling of loss and helplessness through marriage breakup, a child leaving home, loss of job and income, loss of home, and even loss of identity are all areas that healing must be applied to. We take our negative emotions for granted, but sometimes they are the warning signs that Satan is at work. These negative emotions can be nipped in the bud.

The Word of God is the antidote, and when applied, it counters the negative emotion we feel and express. As we begin to confess God's Word over and over, and become one with His Word, His Word begins to grow and then prevail in our lives and circumstances.

So the word of the Lord grew mightily and prevailed (Acts 19:20)

Another area of attack is sex, especially through lustful men. This is where the wisdom of the older widow should not be ignored. The story of Naomi and Ruth is a classic example of the older woman teaching the younger woman how to keep a home (see Titus 2:3-5)

When Ruth chose to go with Naomi to Bethel, there was no record that Naomi had an inkling of hope waiting for her in that country, let alone Ruth. Only that, "...the Lord had visited His people by giving them bread" (Ruth 1:6) Ruth's wise decision to go with her mother-in-law and follow every counsel that she was given by Naomi was what ultimately led her to become the wife of one of the honourable men in Bethel of Judea.

We often only talk about the healing of a wound, forgetting that the cleaning comes before the healing process. I already mentioned how Proverbs 20:30 speaks of the *blueness* of a wound cleansing away evil, as do stripes the inward parts of the belly. The bereaved person's emotional pain needs cleaning before healing can take place.

I woke up with Proverbs 20:30 one morning during a weekend retreat to which I had been invited as a guest speaker in June 2007. I have since understood this Scripture as a flashback to those areas of emotional healing where gaps existed when I was bereaved without realising it. As I meditated on the Scripture, it became obvious to me that, although I seemed to have overcome the pain and could see what the Lord was doing at that time, in actual fact, I had not fully healed.

I believe the deeper the pain, the longer it takes to clean and completely heal emotionally. I have often heard of people ministering healing to the hurting without cleaning the wound beforehand. Giving the hurt person the space to emote in the way he or she chooses, however deeply, creates an environment of relief in the soul.

As this happens, the wound is being cleansed, and this leads on to the healing process. Guidance by an older widow or a professional becomes essential for healing. This also becomes very helpful for the older widow herself, who can now learn to discern her new season and her new role as a guide and mentor, thus finding new purpose for living.

A young widow is often so engrossed in her deep sorrow that she does not see the attack coming upon her children. Often parents cannot separate a child from their behaviour. Therefore, anger or embarrassment or the mixture of both, become the weapons of correction. Worse still, is a situation where the feelings of neglect and isolation become overwhelming leading to a widow instilling this sense of hopelessness and grief in her children.

Such a situation should be a pointer for any widow to become intimate with the Lord, by seeking Him to the exclusion of all else. But she should also seek out healthy relationships that will provide a support network for her. The desire should be to stop looking for God out there and to start listening to God by creating times of meditation and fellowship with the Holy Spirit. Only then will she be able to pass on wholeness to her children.

The Lord will always give meaning and purpose to any situation, however bad it may seem. He may choose to take you out of the situation like He did for Martha and Mary when He raised Lazarus, their brother, from the dead. He may even let you go through loss, like when He allowed His Son, Jesus, to suffer at the hands of sinful men. The Father allowed this to take place so He could have many sons and daughters like you and me.

When Naomi and Ruth left Moab to return to the House of God, the place of bread, they were hoping to find food and possibly shelter. They had no idea that there was not only going to be abundance for Ruth, the young widow who married Boaz, but also permanent provision for Naomi, the older widow. She now had purpose and meaning in life — raising Obed, the grandfather of David. Ruth now had a permanent place in the lineage of our Lord Jesus Christ.

The problem we have is that we believe the lie of Satan that God, the good Lord from whom all blessings flow, is responsible for our loss. When grief comes, Jehovah sees and Jehovah knows, but He is not to be blamed.

Remember to do what Naomi and Ruth did when they returned to God. Do not be like Orpah, who chose to stay in

Moab, the place of loss and bereavement. It is important to note that it is a matter of choice to either turn to God or stay in the place of grief.

"Entreat me not to leave you," said Ruth, but it did not take much persuasion for Orpah to return to Moab (see Ruth 1:16) That is the last we hear of Orpah.

Ruth went on in the Scriptures from the Old Testament through to the New Testament and has the honour of being named in the lineage of our Lord Jesus Christ (see Matt. 1:5)

Scripture does not teach us to forget the dead, though some of us believe so and are probably being taught this in our culture and traditions. Ruth tells us that Boaz acquired Ruth as his wife,

> *...to perpetuate the name of the dead...that the name of the dead may not be cut off from among his brethren and from his position at the gate. (Ruth 4:10)*

It was for the same reason that the Lord killed Onan, the brother of Er who refused to have a proper relationship with his brother's widow, not wanting to have a child for his brother (see Gen. 38:8-10) The Bible says:

> And the thing which he did displeased the Lord; therefore He killed him also. (Genesis 38:10)

Steps to Overcoming Grief

Ask the Lord to give you new interests, because people are designed to give off time-release capsules that they never knew existed within them. You might discover that you have the gift of writing, music, to mentor like Naomi, or defending your rights and the rights of others like the widows, Tamar, and Rizpah (see Luke 18:1-7; Genesis 38:1-30; Matthew 1:3; 2 Samuel 21:1-14)

Seek ways to be a blessing to somebody. Remember the Zarephath widow and the widow with her mite (see 1 Kings 17:8-24; Mark 12:41-44)

Visit places of interests like the theatre, art or science museum, the riverside, libraries, parks, and so on. You might be surprised what you learn and enjoy. And who knows what you might unlock that is inside of you, waiting to be discovered? Those with young children have a tremendous opportunity to develop these interests with and in them as they grow.

Take up new courses. If you have young children, take up family musical lessons together. You might surprise yourself.

Remember King Lemuel, whose mother taught him how to stay away from women and strong drink?

> *The words of King Lemuel, the utterance which his mother taught him: What, my son? And what, son of my womb? And what, son of my vows? Do not give your strength to women, nor your ways to that which destroys kings. It is not for kings, O Lemuel, it is not for kings to drink wine, nor for princes intoxicating drink lest they drink and forget the law, and pervert the justice of all the afflicted* (Proverbs 31:1-5)

I am not sure if his father was alive or dead, but his mother was present to teach him to become a noble man and to remember the afflicted. In the same way, you can invest in your child and spend your energy on worthwhile causes that will yield peaceful and joyful fruits. This is also applicable for the widower.

Redeeming Love

Often, man's disappointments are God's appointments, but we can only discover His purposes in them when we respond in faith. So lean hard on Him and live by faith.

The Song of Solomon is said to be an allegory of Christ's love for His Bride, the Church. As already mentioned, there is a gentle plea of the lover asking his loved one to arise and come with him to the fields because the winter is past and the rains are over. I have often thought of the Book of Ruth as a Cinderella story, and I imagine that this fairy tale is not only true for young girls, but also for widows who may no longer pass easily as a 'young' bride, however young they might be.

The Books of Ruth and Esther are books of true hope and redemption that remind us that fairy tales can only be truly met in God. My plea to young widows or any widow for that matter, is to realise that, with God, there is plenty of redemption. (see Psalm 130:7)

When a widow responds to the wooing of the love of the Lord, there is a fresh lease on life that can only be found in the Lord. The words of Isaiah the prophet become emphatically true:

> ...*and remember no more the reproach of your widowhood. For your Maker is your husband—the Lord Almighty is His name— the Holy One of Israel is your Redeemer; He is called the God of all the earth* (Isaiah 54:4-5 NIV)

If you are a young widow, start dating again when you feel right about it, but not embark on such a course without the help and guidance of a "Naomi".

Consolation

Webster's dictionary defines consolation as "the alleviation of suffering, grief, disappointment, by comforting". This denotes a place of not just coping or adopting good coping mechanisms, but it is a place of overcoming the circumstance. This is a sense of rising above the circumstance and watching with triumph, your victory over the situation that once tried to cripple you.

You say like the psalmist:

But you, O Lord, are a shield for me, my glory and the One who lifts up my head (Psalm 3:3)

This now positions an individual as a life coach, comforting others with the comfort he or she has received from the Father.

Blessed be the God and Father of our Lord Jesus Christ, the Father of mercies and God of all comfort, who comforts us in all our tribulation, that we may be able to comfort those who are in any trouble, with the comfort with which we ourselves are comforted by God. For as the sufferings of Christ abound in us, so our consolation also abounds through Christ. (2 Corinthians 1:3-5)

Depression, as we know it, is one of the most common problems that we face, and it can leave us negative, anxious and hopeless. It usually attaches itself to moments when we are anxious, sad, grieving and facing disappointments in life.

Anxiety in the heart of man causes depression, but a good word makes it glad (Proverbs 12:25)

The path to consolation — the alleviation of suffering,

grief, and disappointments, is to first acknowledge the depression, and then begin to counter it by using God's Word as you think and meditate on it:

> *...whatever things are noble, whatever things are just, whatever things are pure, whatever things are lovely, whatever things are of good report, if there is any virtue and if there is anything praiseworthy — meditate on these things* (Philippians 4:8)

As you meditate on God's Word it becomes a weapon of victory. It is the law (a force) of the Spirit of life in Christ Jesus, which frees you from the law of sin and all that is associated with the fall of man. You are positioned as a victor not as a victim with unhealed or partially healed wounds, but as one who has continued the journey to championship by making holy exchanges. These choices enable you to exchange faith for fear, wholeness for depression and grief, and life for death, as you respond to the love of God.

Consolation, therefore, becomes a reward for "instead of". So, for example, a mother endures the pain of childbirth because of the reward of a child born into our world, and this child is an extension of her.

So you see - consolation is not a coping mechanism but a more-than-conqueror mindset and position. When my daughter, Ruth, was stillborn, I never imagined in my wildest dream that I could ever live a normal life again, let alone comfort others with the comfort I received from the Father. I can now identify with what Paul says in his letter to the Romans:

> *Yet in all these things we are more than conquerors through Him who loved us. For I am persuaded that neither death nor life, nor angels nor principalities nor powers, nor things present nor things to come,*

nor height nor depth, nor any other created thing, shall be able to separate us from the love of God which is in Christ Jesus our Lord. (Romans 8:37-39)

Charles Spurgeon said, "As sure as God puts His children in the furnace, He will be in the furnace with them." I am not sure that He puts us in furnace but I can say with certainty that He permits it, as we see from the story of Job when Satan asked permission to tempt Job into cursing God. The beauty of a 'furnace' experience is that we come out refined.

A Christian lady once told me, during one of my trips to America years ago, that the difference between coal and gold is the degree of heat that is applied and endured. One produces ashes and the other produces brilliance. This is a significant vantage point this refined position gives us to shine and shine for our Lord.

PRAYER:

Heavenly Father, give me the sensitivity to see and experience Your love moving me one step at a time with the practical offers You put in my path to overcome grief. Thank you for the grace to rise up and make my days count in one meaningful way or another and not to succumb to depression, in Jesus Name.

Chapter EIGHT

A Special Group in the House

There is no definite sequence or order in the way that you can serve the widow or the bereaved or the needy. Below are some suggested ways one can go about ministering to the bereaved widow from the early stage of bereavement.

Spend time with the bereaved person.

First, make a telephone call. Then, pay a visit (see James 1:27)

In your visits, talk less. Preferably stay silent, like Job's friends were when they first visited him and saw the terrible condition he was in. (see Job 2:13) You can communicate your sadness through silence. Often when we speak, we say things which are out of turn, which only cause the bereaved more or added hurt. When in doubt of what to say, keep quiet.

As already mentioned, I had a stillborn baby whom we had named Ruth before her birth. Ruth was our first born, and at the time of delivery, my husband was living in Nigeria, awaiting his immigration status to be formalised in order for him join me in the United Kingdom. Ruth arrived dead after a prolonged labour, but I had many Christian friends who came to comfort me. I saw the Lord in everyone who came to comfort me. In fact, there was a Christian friend who heard of my loss at church, and rather than go in for church service, she turned around at the entrance of the church hall, and came straight to visit me. At that point, I remembered the story of the Good Samaritan.

But I also had another close Christian friend at the time who told me that I did not pray enough; hence, my baby died. That seemed a spiritual thing to say at the time, but that one statement almost ruined all the comforts of the Holy Spirit I received from other Christians. I suggest that it is sometimes better to keep quiet than say something. Please do not find silence uncomfortable.

Employ Active Listening Skills

Here are some practical suggestions for those giving comfort:

- Practice active listening. People want their emotions validated. Reflecting a person's pain or anguish can show that you are listening, understanding and sharing in their sad moments and experiences.
- Make eye contact. Try to use gestures like nods and facial expressions.
- Be comfortable with silence. Do not attempt to fill the gaps of silence with words. Express them in tears if need be.

I remember Anne, a community midwife, who was in charge of me during my antenatal visits to the clinic but sadly was not on duty when I went into labour. After Ruth arrived stillborn, she wept a lot with me each time she came to visit me. Anne is Irish, and she was not a friend or even a relative of mine.

At the time, I could not understand, let alone explain, why she wept so much at the death and at the funeral of my baby. One thing I asked the Lord, though, was that the Lord should give Anne to me as a *spiritual baby* in place of Ruth who was now with Him.

I learned from Anne how to mourn with someone who is grieving, without saying words, and for me, that is by far more effective. Job's friends did well by keeping silent with him for the first seven days after they had heard of the deaths of his children and animals, and came to console him.

The Lord answered my prayers. Eight years later, when I gathered myself together to locate the cemetery where Ruth was buried, I heard from Anne with whom I had lost contact. She told me that she is now born again and a follower of the Lord Jesus Christ. You can imagine my joy when we met again in my home and she shared how she became a Christian. Then I knew that all that weeping she did at the time of my loss was the Holy Spirit drawing my attention to something beyond my grief and self, to focus on something eternal — praying for her salvation.

I share this testimony as a tool of how you can turn your grief to the Lord, and He will, in turn, take it and bring beauty out of ashes.

- Allow the bereaved to express their emotions, like anger, frustration at the Lord, fright, anxiety, fears, worries, and so on.
- Do not over spiritualise. Avoid clichés and platitudes such as, "This is God's will, God has a plan," or "All things work together for good." This might not be comforting at the time.
- Be Christ-like. It is a ministry of just being there that says "I am here." Just holding hands and praying within will do at that material time (see James 1:27)
- Offer *practical help* when you visit again.

Be the expected friendly face and do not wait to be asked before you render help. Avoid questions like, "Is it all right to do the laundry?" Simply say, "I am here to do the laundry." This is a closed statement and this leaves her no time to think of refusing the offer.

My sister-in-law shared this point with me, and I have since then found it a very useful and helpful point in our "Befriending a Widow Scheme" we carry out in our ministry.

- Offer to make difficult but necessary calls, like calls to the pastor or friends for the funeral arrangements.
- Do the laundry.
- Do the shopping.
- Do the school runs.
- Spend quality time and make it count.
- Make a note of emotional dates like birthdays, Father's Day, anniversary day etc and make a point to call or even visit.

In summary, try to be a 'Dorcas' (see Acts 9:36-43) Her story is sandwiched between the conversion of Saul of Tarsus, later known as Paul, and the conversion of Cornelius and his household, the first fruits of the Gentile community.

> *At Joppa there was a certain disciple named Tabitha, which is translated Dorcas. This woman was full of good works and charitable deeds which she did. But is happened in those days that she became sick and died. ...And all the widows stood by him weeping, showing the tunics and garments which Dorcas had made while she was with them.* (Acts 9:36-37, 39)

The last verse records that all the widows stood by Peter,

weeping, showing all the good works that Dorcas had rendered to them while she was alive. The bottom line of their plea was for him to raise Dorcas back to life. She was brought back to life and presented to the saints and the widows. Just as Cornelius' good works and prayers brought salvation to him and his household, so Dorcas' good work brought her back to life. This is very note-worthy and gives us much cause for meditation.

> *Let your light so shine before men, that they may see your good works and glorify your Father in heaven* (Matthew 5:16)

Please note that there are some chores that men are best suited to carry out around the home — repairs, painting, servicing the car, mowing the garden... Engage the services of men in these areas.

Pray with the bereaved, if they let you, and fully employ and engage the comfort of the Holy Spirit.

We often forget His role as the Comforter and take it upon ourselves to do and be His role. We are simply vessels and must remember to be available when He needs us. When you visit, if you are in doubt of what to say, then say nothing. Your presence might just be what the bereaved needs.

Be sensitive to the Holy Spirit and to the spirit and mood of the bereaved. For some, the situation may draw them to God, but for others, it may just move them far from God. Still others may refuse to be comforted at all. In that case, retreat and pray for direction. Then visit again.

Peter and the other disciples responded to the Lord's death by going back to fishing. Some bereaved may go back to their old ways or what they used to know before they came to know the Lord. Pray that the Lord will reveal Himself to the bereaved like He appeared to the disciples on the riverbank.

He will show up, for He knows how to reach us wherever and whenever we need Him most. He comes with full provision when we least expect Him.

> *After these things Jesus showed Himself again to the disciples at the Sea of Tiberias, and in this way He showed Himself: ...Jesus said to them, "Come and eat breakfast." Yet none of the disciples dared ask Him, "Who are you?" - knowing that it was the Lord. Jesus then came and took the bread and gave it to them, and likewise the fish.* (John 21:1, 12-13)

I have seen bereaved people who have given in to alcohol and even drug abuse in order to numb the pain of the loss, but this is more common with men. It is common, in my experience, that men find it easier to remarry and do so more quickly.

However deep the pain, God will seek you out just as He did to Peter and the rest of the disciples and restore your confidence in Him and in yourself.

Oh, the unsearchable depth of the riches of His mercy and love toward us!

Emotional and Social Support

There are several ways one can offer emotional and social support to someone who is grieving:

- Visit regularly.
- Encourage the bereaved to express emotion of some kind—such as anger, guilt, or tears — but not to be stuck in that state.

You may well become impatient with the bereaved as she goes on and on in this fashion, but at this stage, expressing emotion of any kind is quite helpful for her in overcoming her pain. Guide her through these emotions. They are not permanent but transitional emotions.

- Help in building new links, interests, and so on.
- Watch for signs of health hazards like sleeplessness, substance abuse like alcohol or drugs to cope with the loss, a state of denial, depression, suicide, and neglect of personal appearance. Encourage her to seek pastoral or professional help if you suspect any of these. We had an occasion of working with a young widow who began to show some of these signs, and we immediately sought professional help for her.
- Do not take anger or irritability directed at you, personally; as such emotions are all part of the grieving process.

Please note that there are some additional high-risk factors, which may cause grief to last longer with some than others. This could be as a result of the following:

- Sudden or unexpected death
- Unexplained death
- Death with stigmas like poison, suicide
- Death involving murder, inquest, or legal proceedings
- More than one death in the family
- History of mental health problems
- Low self-esteem
- Poor social or family support.

In such cases, please seek medical and professional help and I would recommend that a huge support network should be available to any such individual.

PRAYER:

Heavenly Father, help me seek out help when I feel I need some and if I am too helpless to seek help, please send Your help my way. Give me grace to accept and receive it when you send it, in Jesus Name.

Chapter NINE

It Is A Family Affair

The role of the church in the care of the bereaved, single parents, widows and widowers cannot be ignored. Caring for these groups of people is a vital part of the Church's ministry and is based upon strong biblical principles. This is a matter that concerns everyone, especially those in the Body of Christ.

Isaiah commands us to relieve the oppressed, defend the fatherless and plead the cause of widows (see Isaiah 1:17,23) It is quite shocking to note that, through the prophet Isaiah, the Lord classified the neglect of the oppressed, widows and the fatherless alongside the sins of idolatry and adultery.

The provisions to look after these groups of people are to be taken from the storehouse, as we read in Deuteronomy:

> *At the end of every third year you shall bring out the tithe of your produce of that year and store it up within your gates. And the Levite, because he has no portion nor inheritance with you, and the stranger and the fatherless and the widow who are within your gates, may come and eat and be satisfied, that the Lord your God may bless you in all the work of your hand which you do.* (Deuteronomy 14:28-29)

According to this Scripture, these target groups (Levites, strangers, fatherless and widows) should have their needs supplied out of the tithes given to the local church. Every third year, or every third month of the year, the tithes should be used to bless these people.

Following the Law of Moses which mandates provision for the fatherless, strangers, and widows, the apostles in Acts had a daily distribution in place for the widows.

Unfortunately, they neglected the Grecian widows at first. However, this was immediately put right by the apostles once it was brought to their attention.

> *Now in those days, when the number of the disciples was multiplying, there arose a complaint against the Hebrews by the Hellenists, because their widows were neglected in the daily distribution. Then the twelve summoned the multitude of the disciples and said, "It is not desirable that we should leave the word of God and serve tables. Therefore, brethren, seek out from among you seven men of good reputation, full of the Holy Spirit and wisdom, whom we may appoint over this business; but we will give ourselves continually to prayer and to the ministry of the word"* (Acts 6:1-4)

Here we see it is the responsibility of pastors and leaders to appoint people who will oversee the business of making provision for the needy in the local church.

Immediately before the *widow's mite* account, the Lord Jesus warned us to beware of the scribes who love the best seats for the pretext of making long prayers but *devour* widows' houses. We do not have to go very far to find this situation prevailing in our churches today. If we simply swap the word "scribe" for "teacher or preacher" of the Word, then we soon find out that we cannot point the finger too far away from ourselves.

We find the same account in Mark:

> *Then He said to them in His teaching, "Beware of the scribes, who desire to go around in long robes, love greetings in the marketplaces, the best seats in the synagogues, and the best places at feasts, who devour widows' houses, and for pretence make long prayers. These will receive greater condemnation"* (Mark 12:38-40)

Providing on Purpose

A young African widow who is now serving in our ministry and also heading-up the young people's department, told me how the local church she used to attend, insisted she contribute a large sum of money to a church building fund. They did this even though the church knew she was an asylum-seeker with no recourse to public funds whatsoever. In the end she had to leave that church because they continued to pester her for this contribution.

This is the insensitivity to the needs of widows or any needy person in a local church that the Lord talks about in the story mentioned above.

Have a structure in place for the care of widows in your local church. God Himself fosters a special interest in the widows, even calling Himself their defender (see Psalm 68:5; 146:9) He uttered the severest denunciations against those who defraud and oppress them (see Psalm 94:6; Ezekiel 22:7; Malachi 3:5)

With regards the remarriage of widows, the only restriction imposed by the Mosaic Law refers to that widow who is left childless. In that case, the brother of the deceased husband has an obligation to marry her (see Deuteronomy 25:5-6; Matt. 22:23-30) In some parts of Africa, this is still done in some cultures.

It is obvious from Scripture that widows could remarry, as we see in the case of Ruth.

A wife is bound by law as long as her husband lives; but if her husband dies, she is at liberty to be married to whom she wishes, only in the Lord. (1 Corinthians 7:39)

It is important that we bear in mind that, although our emphasis is on care for the widows, this must not be at the exclusion of orphans and strangers, single parents, and any other needy in our midst. We see that several Scriptures mention all three groups, including the Levites, as people the Church should care for. Disobedience in this area is regarded as sin through the eyes of prophets like Isaiah, Jeremiah, Ezekiel, and even by the so-called *minor prophets* like Zechariah and Malachi.

The word "widow" is mentioned over eighty times in the Bible, fifteen times together with "the fatherless". Widows and the fatherless receive more focus in the New Testament than orphans. The entire Book of Ruth is dedicated to widows; Ruth, Naomi, and Orpah. I believe that God our Father is so passionate about widows and His care for them is obvious throughout Scripture.

Here is a list of verses that might interest you to take time out and read.

The prophet Ezekiel listed this neglect or mistreatment of strangers, the fatherless, and widows as one of the sins in Israel:

> *In you they have made light of father and mother; in your midst they have oppressed the stranger; in you they have mistreated the fatherless and the widow.* (Ezekiel 22:7)

Furthermore, Ezekiel — prophesying about the sins of Israel in his time — mentions that the sins of Sodom: pride, fullness of food, abundance of idleness, and not strengthening the hand of the poor and needy were as abominable as the sins of Israel (see Ezekiel 16:49)

The Lord judged the sins of Sodom, and one of these is the neglect of the poor and needy. We do know He feels the same way now as He felt then.

1 Timothy 5:3-16 gives us guidelines for putting a system in place for the poor and needy:

- Believers should take care of the widows in their households.
- The local church should take care of widows who are poor and alone in the world, if they are serving the Lord.
- The widow in the church who is sixty or over is the responsibility of the church.

In our day, there are many destitute young widows and single parents who are struggling with their children's upbringing through no fault of their own. For many, the story is the same; their husbands have abandoned them for other women. I believe that it the responsibility of the Church to treat each case with the merit it deserves, by looking into each case critically.

In the Book of Acts, the apostles had the responsibility of looking after the widows. I believe that it was simply an oversight that the Greek widows were neglected. As soon as the complaint was brought to their attention, an immediate action was taken by appointing deacons to right this wrong.

They chose seven men filled with the Holy Spirit and faith. Among those were Stephen, the first martyr in the New Testament Church, and Philip, who had no need for an airplane to evangelise as he was simply caught up by the Holy Spirit to go from one place to another to minister the gospel.

I am convinced by this account that it is not just the women who have the duty to take on the responsibility to care for the widows or the needy, just as it is not only a woman's role to be an intercessor in the Body of Christ.

I also believe that the cry for revival in the Church can also be found in this account in the Bible. Here, we are told that the apostles responded to the cry from the Grecian widows, and the result was the increased spread and impact of the Word of God.

> *And the saying pleased the whole multitude. And they chose Stephen, a man full of faith and the Holy Spirit, and Philip, Prochorus, Nicanor, Timon, Parmenas, and Nicolas, a proselyte from Antioch, whom they set before the apostles; and when they had prayed, they laid hands on them. Then the word of God spread, and the number of disciples multiplied greatly in Jerusalem, and a great many of the priests were obedient to the faith.* (Acts 6:5-7)

For a great many of us, we live in a society where the Bible is interpreted to suit modern-day lifestyles and political correctness at the great expense of what the Bible actually says and means.

We also see interpretations and perversions of our faith by 'ministers' who have a form of religion but deny the power of our Lord Jesus and the power of the Holy Spirit.

Most times, it is little things — like the rudder of a ship, the bit in a horse's mouth or the light of a match — which have a huge impact and result. Do you suppose the apostles thought that, by responding to such a little complaint, these results would take place?

Then the word of God spread, and the number of disciples multiplied greatly... (Acts 6:7)

This has been written down for our instruction, for us to pay heed so we can expect revival in the Church.

On the Cross, as our Lord was dying, He remembered to hand the care of His mother to John, the beloved, and not to His brothers and sisters who at this time had not acknowledged Him (Jesus) as the Son of God.

It is quite interesting to note that "widows", not orphans, receive the most attention in the New Testament, except in James 1:27. This is in contrast to the emphasis on other groups like "orphans, strangers, and Levites" in the Old Testament.

Orphans, widows, and strangers, especially widows are, in my experience, the most marginalised members of our present-day Church.

Luke, the physician, speaks about the Widow of Nain, the widow and her mite, and the importunate widow (see Luke 7:11-17; 21:1-4; 18:1-7)

The Lord used this importunate widow to illustrate persistent and prevailing prayer and to command that we ought always to pray and not to faint.

I am convinced that, after mentioning widows over eighty times in the Word of God, with so many of those times in the

New Testament, this is not an issue the Lord wants the Church to ignore or marginalise. However few the widows might be in a local church, they should be acknowledged and given recognition in the church. Like a little rudder in a ship, they are vital to the Body of Christ.

Not Forsaken

One day, as I was praying, asking the Lord to please give widows recognition in the Church, I heard clearly in my spirit this statement: "The Church is the Bride of Christ, but I am the Husband to the widow." I drew strength and hope from this statement as I linked this with Isaiah 54:

> *Do not fear, for you will not be ashamed; neither be disgraced, for you will not be put to shame; for you will forget the shame of your youth, and will not remember the reproach of your widowhood any more. For your Maker is your husband, the Lord of hosts is His name; and your Redeemer is the Holy One of Israel; He is called the God of the whole earth.* (Isaiah 54:4-5)

It may appear that the Lord has forsaken the widow like it seemed He had done with the Israelites, but it is only for a small moment. The Lord promises the widow that she shall not remember the reproach of her widowhood any more, for her Creator, the Lord of hosts, is her Husband. He is known as the God of the whole earth. I appreciate that Bible scholars may have differing opinions about this chapter, but for this context, a literal meaning will suffice.

It is interesting to note that in the Old Testament, the widows are often mentioned alongside the fatherless, strangers, and Levites. But in the New Testament, the other groups, not the widows, receive no further attention.

This is surely not a group that the Lord wants the Church to ignore. The Lord Jesus Himself, made constant reference to widows. In case you are wondering whether God cares for only the widows in the Church, the Lord Jesus reminds us in Luke that there were many widows in Israel, yet Elijah was sent to a widow in Zarephath in the city of Sidon — a Gentile city (see Luke 4:25-26)

When the Lord Jesus mentioned this, those in the Synagogue rose up to thrust Him out of the city for exposing their hard-heartedness. This is a cry to reach any needy widow or single parent, but we must begin in the Household of Faith — the Church.

Isaiah 58 tells us that to fast is acceptable to God; to give your bread to the hungry, bring those poor without shelter into your home, and to clothe the naked (see Isaiah 58:7)

Often, the widow is found in one or more of the categories just mentioned. We cannot ignore compassion, and expect the Lord to hear us when we cry out in our day of trouble. Interestingly, some ray of hope is beginning to shine through.

Doors that were once shut to the plea to support widows are beginning to open, and the widows are beginning to receive recognition. An older widow in our ministry shared early this year about how she visited her home country and shared this ministry vision with the king of her tribe. The king not only caught the vision but gave a Christmas provision to over fifty widows in his village that would last them for a long time.

In the same chapter of Isaiah, God's comfort to the widows is also extended to the divorced and the single parent:

"For the Lord has called you like a woman forsaken and grieved in spirit, like a youthful wife when you were refused," says your God. "For a mere moment I have forsaken you, but with great mercies I will gather you. With a little wrath I hid my face from you for a moment; but with everlasting kindness I will have mercy on you," says the Lord, your Redeemer. (Isaiah 54:6-8)

The divorced — the young wife forsaken by her husband — receives treatment strikingly similar to God's perpetual covenant of kindness with Israel. The rate of divorce in the Body of Christ is alarming, yet God will remember the widow and the woman forsaken and grieved in spirit, with great mercies.

- **Appoint deacons to take on the care of widows.**

The first soup kitchen is mentioned in the Book of Acts — daily distribution of food (see Acts 6:1-7) This caused many to come to know the Lord. Today, this could be a monthly offering for widows with financial needs, especially those with children.

Scripture commands that the tithes should be used for the Levites, widows, fatherless, and strangers. Paul instructs us to be responsible for the widows in our households, so that the church can take care of the widows who are without relatives. (see 1 Timothy 5:3-16)

It is the role of every Christian to visit the widows and the orphans in their time of affliction (see James 1:27) It should not be left to a selected few, although the responsibility for this task should be given to appointed persons, as found in the early church.

- **Encourage "Naomi and Ruth" relationships.**

    Let the older widows mentor the younger widows, as we find in the Book of Ruth.

    Naomi's instruction to Ruth is quite deep and rich when viewed from a spiritual stand-point (see Ruth 3:3) I find the following commentary by Pat Chen, in the Women of Destiny Bible, to be very helpful:

    - Wash yourself — with the water of the Word and a lifestyle of repentance and forgiveness (see Ephesians. 5:26)
    - Anoint yourself — by spending time in His presence in prayer, praise and worship.
    - Put on your best clothes of righteousness, holiness, humility, right motives and attitudes — adorn yourself with a meek and quiet spirit:

    Do not let your adornment be merely outward—arranging the hair, wearing gold, or putting on fine apparel— rather let it be the hidden person of the heart, with the incorruptible beauty of a gentle and quiet spirit, which is very precious in the sight of God (1 Peter 3:3-4)

    Go down to the threshing floor — because you are made of dust. Let God do His sifting work in you. A place of sifting and separation would lead to a place of recognition and honour. (see Ruth 3:11)

    We know that this worked for Ruth and it can work for anyone who takes this on board.

    This, of course, can also be looked at from a physical perspective. The widow, especially a young widow, should be encouraged to put off her widow garments — a symbol of forgetting the past and adorning herself in preparation for remarriage.

But Scripture commands that they must marry in the Lord, as already mentioned earlier in the book.

- Do not render a stereotype or blanket service for every widow.

Each widow has her own special needs. Be patient when a widow finds it hard or is slow to overcome bereavement. This is because widowhood evokes strong emotions like anger, rage, frustration, and even guilt. As we target the individual need of a widow, it becomes a lot easier to deal with the issue of bereavement. Therefore, you are positioned to help and come alongside her on the road to recovery from her loss.

- Target the individual need.

Different people shut down for various reasons. Below are some examples:

- Tamar, the widow of Er son of Judah, desired a child (see Gen. 38)
- Rizpah, Saul's concubine widow, desired a proper burial for her sons. This act led to the healing of the land (see 2 Samuel 21:10-14)
- The Zarephath widow wanted a continual supply of food for her and her son (see 1 Kings 17:8-16)
- Naomi desired to return to her country and town— Bethel, meaning the "House of Bread"—and to the Land of Judah, meaning "Praise" (see Ruth 1:1-8)
- Ruth desired to be with her mother-in-law and her God. She found a home and her destiny (see Ruth 3:1)
- The widow with the two sons needed a financial breakthrough for her sons not to go into slavery (see 2 Kings 4:1-7)

- The importunate widow needed vengeance against her enemies (see Luke 18:1-7)
- The Widow of Nain needed a miracle that she thought was impossible. She was not even looking for one (see Luke 7:11-17)

• Take a note of emotional dates — birthdays, Father's Day, anniversary dates, and the kind.

Let the bereaved know that someone is always at the other end of the line. Select a "support person watch" for the widow — preferably the person she warmed up to during initial visits. Ensure the person stays in touch, even up to a year later. Somehow, you will know when to exit your role, but the support must be ongoing.

• Organise trainings, workshops, and seminars to handle personal issues and affairs

- Loneliness
- Low self-esteem and lack of confidence
- Parenting and taking up dual roles
- Hope for the future
- Finances
- Overcoming bereavement and depression, the list goes on and on.

Create a support network for widows.

- Encourage regular meetings for widows where possible. This will avoid isolation, depression, and other related emotional illness that may arise from the loss of a spouse.
- Create a committee of men who can handle minor needs around her home, addressing things from a

leaking bathroom sink to minor drainage work.
- Create a transportation network involving others in the church that can help widows, especially older widows, with transportation needs.
- Create an emergency fund to meet unexpected repair needs and financial needs.
- Help widows to find ways to use their skills and talents in ministry opportunities in the church and through the church to the community.

As the widow is empowered, she can take her rightful place of honour in the Kingdom of God through hands-on ministry opportunities.

This support framework will guard this silent community and free them to be the army they truly are in the Body of Christ.

Here is a story to conclude this chapter in the best way I can think of. One day, I was hunting for a second hand car with our daughter, Salome. After a long day of an unsuccessful trip to another town, I insisted that we make one more stop at a local car garage that I had been visiting several weeks before.

On our way to the car garage, we hit the evening traffic with fast drivers trying to cut lanes. One such driver attempted to do just that and my gracious daughter let him in our lane. With irritation, I looked at her and said to her that she should have 'let someone else' let that driver in their lane as we were in a hurry to get to the car garage.

She gently turned her head and said to me - "I am that someone else." Let us be the person that someone else can count on when the need arises.

PRAYER:

Heavenly Father, may I always be that 'someone' that You can count on to come along and help someone in this journey of life. May I not be too busy or too bugged down with religion not to see that a wounded person needs my help, however small the help I can offer, in Jesus Name.

Chapter **TEN**

The Unsung Army

I believe that there are various types of needs which widows present and represent. In the Bible, each need not only tells a story, but is built into an account that changes the lives and re-writes history for them and for us. The underpinning factor in each of these is the situation of loss and widowhood, yet each has a need besides the loss.

This has consigned each story to the pages of the Bible. I call them the V.I.L. — Very Important Ladies, who acted bravely, regardless of their vulnerable state. I pray that, as you look at each of these stories, you will find something that the Lord wants you to see.

This is not just for the widows, but for any reader, and, of course, the Church, the Body of Christ. I believe this will enable us to avoid a blanket service and carefully look at and meet the needs that each individual widow presents. This list is by no means exhaustive, but is only some of the categories or types of widows that I have drawn out from biblical accounts whenever I have heard a preacher make the reference.

The Desperate Widow

Tamar was the widow of Er, the son of Judah. Her account is found in Genesis:

Then Judah took a wife for Er his first-born, and her name was Tamar. (Gen. 38:6)

She gave birth to twin boys called Perez and Zerah. Tamar is mentioned again in Ruth 4:12 when the elders were blessing Boaz at his marriage to Ruth.

Tamar, the first widow to be mentioned in the Bible, was desperate. More than any other widow mentioned, it seems she was absolutely driven by desperation to a place of reckless abandon. She abandoned her dignity, forgot protocols, and fought for her destiny. She had to fight against the deception of her father-in-law.

Tamar found her way into the Bible by taking off her mourning clothes. She had discovered that Judah, her father-in-law, had tricked her by sending her home after the death of his two sons. She needed wisdom to regain her place and bear a child.

The shrewd method she employed to fulfil the law, received praise even from Judah when he found out that he had fathered the child she was carrying. You will probably agree with me that God approved of her — she positioned herself in the lineage of our Lord Jesus Christ. (see Matt. 1:3)

The Determined Widow

Rizpah, the concubine widow of King Saul, brought

healing to her land when she stayed out in the open to protect the dead from the birds of the air and the beasts of the field. She showed kindness to the dead and, consequently, healed her land, once her actions were brought to the knowledge of King David (see 2 Sam. 21:1-14).

Now Rizpah the daughter of Aiah took sackcloth and spread it for herself on the rock, from the beginning of harvest until the late rains poured on them from heaven. And she did not allow the birds of the air to rest on them by day or the beasts of the field by night. (2 Samuel 21:10)

When a land is cursed, the effect is soon felt by all. A lack of rain results in drought and famine in the land. The lack of rain in Israel for three years led King David to seek the Lord for its cause. The Lord revealed the cause, leading David to put things right by killing some members of King Saul's family, to repay the wrong King Saul committed against the Gibeonites.

This led King David to take the necessary steps toward burying the dead, including King Saul and his son, Jonathan, who had received no proper burial at the time of their death. Their bones had been held by the men of Jabesh Gilead.

Rizpah's desire to see that her sons' remains were not left to the birds of the air or the beasts of the fields, brought an end to the reproach on the household of Saul and Jonathan. After this whole exercise, the Lord healed the land.

Who would have thought that an act of a widow would lift a curse from a nation and bring healing to the land of a whole nation?

If you are still in doubt that this silent community is an army in the Body of Christ, I hope that this and the next account will help eliminate that.

The Widow Who Heard God

The most frequently mentioned widow by ministers of the Gospel is the widow of Zarephath. (see 1 Kings 17:8-15)

Then the word of Lord came to him, saying, "Arise, go to Zarephath, which belong to Sidon, and dwell there. See, I have commanded a widow there to provide for you." (1 Kings 17:8-9)

Does this account only involve the dimension of giving to the man of God or the church, despite abject poverty, or is there more to this account than meets the eye?

The man of God was sent to the widow by God to ask to be fed because, as a prophet, he heard from God. We hear nothing about the widow who also heard from God directly. The Scripture clearly states that God had commanded a widow to provide for the prophet Elijah. If the widow had not heard from God, I am not sure if the prophet Elijah would have had very much success with her.

I have often wondered how this Gentile widow, who had no connection with the Jewish race, heard from God, but I am content with the fact that Scripture records that she heard from God and obeyed, even though it took a little reassurance and persuasion from Elijah. Her obedience to this instruction brought food to her and her son that lasted throughout the famine.

I believe that what you hear the Lord say to you will often, but not always, be confirmed by external sources. This could also happen the other way around — God could confirm a message you hear from others.

The Debtor Widow

The widow with the jar of oil cried out to Elisha in desperation, not only out of poverty, but also out of the fear of losing her sons to slavery. (see 2 Kings 4:1-7)

> *A certain woman of the wives of the sons of the prophets cried out to Elisha, saying, "Your servant my husband is dead, and you know that your servant feared the Lord. And the creditor is coming to take my two sons to be his slaves."* (2 Kings 4:1)

She needed to pay her debt or her sons would be sold into slavery. Here was a woman who was a widow of one of the sons of the prophets and very obviously known to Elisha. She reminded Elisha that his servant, her husband, had feared the Lord. It sounds to me as if she was reminding the Lord that the time to reward faithfulness had come. And if not at that critical point of need, then when?

We are told in the New Testament that God remembered Cornelius for his prayers and alms. This widow knew how to make withdrawals from her late husband's deposit of faithfulness with God. The thought of losing sons to slavery is heart breaking for any mother. At her most crucial time of need, this widow remembered to call on the Lord.

I believe that there are some situations that you are not designed to deal with alone. It may require a chain of people and actions to make a miracle happen in a situation. This widow remembered to draw on the anointing of Elisha in her desperate moment, and this brought her a miracle.

There is also a lesson which cannot be overlooked — obeying and following instructions in the relationship you have with the person the Lord has connected you with in your local church. The Bible says to believe His prophets and you will be successful. (see 2 Chronicles 20:20)

The Emigrant Widow

In the Book of Ruth, we have a story of sadness, hopelessness and utter loss which culminates into one of the most wonderful stories of hope, redemption, and a blissful ending. If you think this story is too good to be true, you are not the only one. Some folks kept passing over this unbelievable yet true story, and it carries on into the New Testament.

The lineage of our Lord Jesus is traced right back to a young Moabite widow, Ruth, who found love with the wealthiest man in town. She chose to commit to an older widow, Naomi, her mother-in-law. Neither Naomi's husband nor her sons, now grown and married, were dead. When Naomi heard that the Lord had visited His people with bread again and she decided to return to her country, her daughter-in-law, Ruth, chose to go with her to the land of Judah.

> *Then she arose with her daughters-in-law that she might return from the country of Moab, for she had heard in the country of Moab that the Lord had visited His people by giving them bread. Therefore she went out from the place where she was, and her two daughters-in-law with her; and they went on the way to return to the land of Judah.* (Ruth 1:6-7)

The choice to leave the place of idolatry, and return to the God of Israel, brought about a lasting legacy for both widows. This singular act not only changed Naomi's life and helped her to become a fulfilled woman in her old age, but it also helped her daughter-in-law, Ruth, to remarry and live on into the pages of the New Testament. Naomi's life is one of the Bible's beautiful tales of redemption. She learned that it is never too late for God to redeem any situation.

The Redeemed Widow

Ruth followed and clung to Naomi, and she found love and a home in Judah. She not only found love, she found the redeeming Love of God. As we are aware, God is all about love — redeeming love. The lessons to be learned from this young widow will help many to fulfil their destiny as they follow the steps that Naomi gave Ruth to seek a marriage partner (see Ruth 3)

When you come to know that your life the one piece of a large jigsaw puzzle without which the whole picture is incomplete, then you will appreciate that God's purpose for you is intimately linked to His whole purpose for creation.

A young widow showed an unforgettable act of kindness to me about three years ago. I had just been appointed a parent governor of our daughters' school and had to attend an induction course in another part of the city.

We had just finished a local radio show where we were raising the profile of our ministry, and I had no clue where the induction course was to take place. My wonderful young friend drove with me to help me locate this place. I tried to tell the Christian sister who gave us a ride in her car that I could manage from where I was, but my friend knew, no matter how hard I tried to disguise my confusion, that I was completely lost. She offered to ride further with me, and somehow, we found the place. My young friend stayed with me the whole time and sat outside in the cold for over two hours on an empty stomach while I attended my course.

When I asked her why she did it, she said that she figured that if I got lost, I would not be stranded alone. "At least you would have me with you."

As we drove home the story of Ruth flooded my mind, and I wondered what would make someone sacrifice herself for me in such a fashion. I have no answer and still do not have one, except to pray that this labour of love will not go unrewarded.

Like Ruth, my young friend understood what it means to be there for somebody. When Ruth chose to be there for Naomi, did she know that she would gain the Lord's favour in a huge way? Hardly... But the Scriptures said of her that she was a virtuous woman.

> *Then he said, "Blessed are you of the Lord, my daughter! For you have shown more kindness at the end that at the beginning, in that you did not go after young men, whether poor or rich. And now, my daughter, do not fear. I will do for you all that you request, for all the people of my town know that you are a virtuous woman."* (Ruth 3:10-11)

Ruth is the only woman recorded in the Bible as a, virtuous woman, in answer to the question: "Who can find a virtuous wife?" (Proverbs 31:10) She truly was worth more than her weight in gold. Her worth was far above rubies, and the Lord bestowed honour on her for her ethics and commitment to a covenant relationship with Naomi, to her land, to her people, and to her God.

The Widow Who Clung to Her Past

Also found in the Book of Ruth, is the account of another young widow, Orpah, who chose to hang on to her past.

> *Then they lifted up their voices and wept again; and Orpah kissed her mother-in-law, but Ruth clung to her. And she said, "Look, your sister-in-law has gone back to her people and to her gods..."* (Ruth 1:14-15)

Orpah had the same opportunity as Ruth to go with Naomi to the land of Judah, but she (Orpah) chose to return to Moab where she knew grief. She probably felt that it was pointless to hang around Naomi, especially now that Naomi was going to her own country which was unfamiliar territory for her. Sadly, nothing is mentioned about her in Scripture after she kissed Naomi goodbye.

Oftentimes, our tendency is to mistake a temporary condition for a permanent state. I believe that widowhood is only a temporary condition, not a permanent state, especially if you are only sixty years old or younger.

There are widows who refuse to be either comforted or see past their immediate season of loss. If they do not venture into the future, however uncertain, they will just remain in the place of pain. Sadly, some widows can embrace this temporary season and fail to see past it. This is exactly what Orpah did when she failed to press on with Naomi like her sister-in-law Ruth.

> *And now abide faith, hope, love, these three; but the greatest of these is love.* (1 Corinthians 13:13)

We underestimate the power of Hope, because it receives less emphasis in the church compared to Love and Faith. Love gives birth to Hope and then Faith. However bleak the lack of a future with Naomi seemed, Ruth's fervent love for her fuelled her hope and moved her into a place of faith that worked tremendously for her.

On the contrary, Orpah did not perceive hope in going with Naomi to a land and a future she was unsure of. Hence, she returned.

We need all three of these ingredients in our walk with the Lord, even more so when we experience bereavement or find ourselves in situations that seem totally hopeless. Our loved ones or good memories may be in our past, but we do not have to stay in or hold on to the past. Trials come to all, and our reaction defines us. The purpose of this book is to enable you to shed your past and embrace the future with Hope.

The Prophetic Widow

Anna's account is found in Luke 2. She was eighty-four and had been married for only seven years when her husband died. She remained a widow for the rest of her life.

> *Now there was one, Anna, a prophetess, the daughter of Phanuel, of the tribe of Asher. She was of great age, and had lived with a husband seven years from her virginity; and this woman was widow of about eighty-four years, who did not depart from the temple, but served God with fasting and prayers night and day.* (Luke 2:36-37)

Anna spent her time in the house of the Lord, fasting and praying night and day. What drove a young lady, now old, to serve the Lord in this manner? This could only be a response to what she perceived in her spirit, and through the Holy Spirit, about the coming Messiah.

She was not from the tribe of Judah or Levi, but from a tribe hardly mentioned in the Bible — the tribe of Asher. When she responded to what she perceived in her spirit with prayer and fasting, the Bible refers to her as 'prophetess' and she had the wonderful privilege of praying through and seeing the birth of the Messiah.

Scriptures seem to indicate that Anna made her home in the temple, dedicating herself to the service of the Lord with prayer and fasting night and day, until she saw the fulfilment of the birth of the Messiah. She then spoke of the Messiah to all those who looked for redemption in Jerusalem.

The need for her type in the Church and especially in a local church cannot be overemphasised.

There is an elderly lady from Uganda who served in the ministerial cabinet of her country but came to the United Kingdom in the 1980s as an asylum seeker because of the Idi Amin regime. She attended Kensington Temple in Nottinghill Gate, London, before my sister, Rose, and I arrived in the United Kingdom and also joined the church.

It was reported that she spent her time in the church praying over the empty seats, calling people from the north, south, east, and west of the world. Before long, there was an influx of peoples from all over the world. By the early 1990s, the church recorded 110 nationalities worshipping together, with four services held every Sunday.

Years later, when this elderly widow made her periodic visits to Kensington Temple, my sister and I got to meet her. The then senior pastor, Reverend Wynne Lewis, admitted that the revival in the church was as a result of this praying widow. She saw beyond the empty chairs and called "...those things which do not exist as though they did." (Romans 4:17)

I believe that a praying widow is a prophetic widow. Once

the Church begins to give place and recognition to a widow who is available to pray, we will see God's Kingdom manifested in our churches.

My spiritual mentor in Holland once told me that just as Anna, the prophetess in the Bible, was maintained by the provision from the temple, the Church today should do the same with the praying elderly widows in order to see God's will birthed in our community and in our city. I totally agree and I hope you agree too.

The Intercessory Widow

The importunate widow's story in Luke 18 is widely used in the Church to illustrate the persistence in prayer.

Now there was a widow in that city; and she came to him saying, "Get justice for me from my adversary." And he would not for a while; but afterward he said within himself, "Though I do not fear God nor regard man, yet because this widow troubles me I will avenge her, lest by her continual coming she weary me." (Luke 18:3-5)

In this story, the Lord Jesus Christ commands that we ought always to pray and not to faint. He teaches us persistence in prayer, using a widow to illustrate His point.

There is definitely something in a widow or her bereaved condition to which the Lord relates in His ministry of prayer. Hebrews 7:25 tells us that He lives to make intercession for us. Intercession is the current and continual ministry of our Lord Jesus Christ for the Church, His Body, as He is seated at the Father's right hand in Heaven.

How like the Lord to use foolish things to confound the wise and the weak things to confound the mighty! Who would think that a widow in her vulnerable and helpless state would wield such enormous power to change her circumstances and her world?

The Church has a habit of detaching itself from situations and circumstances that are not glamorous. Yet the Bible tells us that members of the body, who seem to be weaker, less honourable, and less presentable, have greater modesty. (see 1 Corinthians 12:20-26) God has composed the body in such a way that when one part suffers, all the parts suffer with it; so, we should care for one another. If this is true of members of physical body, how much more so the Body of Christ?

The importunate widow displayed courage, determination and perseverance. She boldly approached the judge who did not fear God nor regard man. She gave him no rest until she was avenged on her enemy.

This judge did not exhibit the fear of the Lord, yet he was used to meet the need of this widow. How often we limit our God, even though we know He can use anyone, even kings, to advance His Kingdom here on earth! Isaiah 45:1-4 tells us that the Lord chose for His purpose a gentile king, King Cyrus, even before his birth. Proverbs 21:1 tells us that the king's heart is in the Lord's hand, and He turns it in any direction He chooses.

This type of widow will not cease praying until she brings in the Will and Purpose of God on earth. I wonder if the Lord had Tamar and Ruth in mind as He shared this parable — particularly Tamar, who let nothing stand in her way in making sure that the inheritance law of marriage was justly served.

The Bereaved Widow

The account of the Widow of Nain who lost her only son is heartrending and seemingly beyond hope:

And when He came near the gate of the city, behold, a dead man was being carried out, the only son of his mother; and she was a widow. And a large crowd from the city was with her. When the Lord saw her, He had compassion on her and said to her, "Do not weep." Then He came and touched the open coffin, and those who carried him stood still. And He said, "Young man, I say to you, arise." So he who was dead sat up and began to speak. And He presented him to his mother. (Luke 7:12-15)

The Lord met her at the city gate as the funeral procession of her only son was being led out. Note the immediate reaction of our Lord Jesus Christ when He saw her. Without being asked, He approached her and told her not to weep. He proceeded to raise the young man from the dead and presented him to his mother.

Peter did the same thing when He raised Dorcas from the dead — he presented her to the disciples and the widows.

Contrast this widow with the importunate widow we just discussed. The bereaved widow did not need to go and ask for help like the importunate widow. The Lord saw and reached out to her, because her situation was one of double tragedy.

No two bereavement situations are alike, and, therefore, ministry to the bereaved should always be individually tailored. The guiding and ruling factor in the Lord Jesus' life and ministry was, and still is, compassion, and this should be our motivating factor too. When an individual or the Church is moved by compassion, then we show that the Kingdom of God is manifest.

Then fear came upon all, and they glorified God, saying, "A great prophet has risen up among us"; and, "God has visited His people." (Luke 7:16)

The Tithing Widow

The poor widow and her mite is a heart-warming story which draws out from us a depth of compassion on one hand, and cries out against injustice, on the other (see Mark 12:41-44) This is especially true in relation to the Lord's rebuke against those

> ...who devour widows' houses, and for pretence make long prayers... (Mark 12:40)

The prophet Ezekiel, in pointing out the sins of Israel, says:

> In you they have made light of father and mother; in your midst they have oppressed the stranger; in you they have mistreated the fatherless and the widow. (Ezekiel 22:7)

Mark 12 is not just a lesson on sacrificial giving, as we have been taught over the years. The Lord Jesus is actually shining a spotlight on and revealing to His followers that the widow is being exploited, while out of her poverty she has given all that she has. What would make a poor widow give her last farthing — all her living?

I believe that this kind of deep devotion could only come from deep reverence for God and His Word, not just loyalty to the system of the day; the synagogue, whose leaders make long prayers in pretence and 'devour widows' houses'.

This kind of intimacy with God and complete trust in Him defies explanation and even comprehension. Her farthing may not even be noticed in the church offering, but it certainly earned her a place in the pages of the Bible. The Lord Jesus saw and recognised a widow amidst the crowd — one who is usually invisible and voiceless in the Church — and made a point of drawing the disciples' attention to her and her act. She teaches us a valuable lesson in giving. She parallels the Zarephath widow, who gave her last meal to the prophet Elijah.

I have had first hand experience with a young widow, whom I have mentioned earlier in this book, who spent her very small state benefit on my husband and me when we had just stepped into full-time ministry. On one occasion, she paid for me to take my husband to a restaurant for his birthday while she looked after our young children for the evening. I believe a widow knows when she hears from God to bless a servant of God or anybody else, and she will obey the Lord.

I had a dream on February 2, 2001. In this dream, I observed many people standing outside watching the sky. I noticed in the sky that there was a horse which appeared to be sitting at the feet of a lion. But as I looked closely, there appeared to be five horses.

Many others joined me and we stood gazing at the sky, watching what was going on. Someone in the crowd said that there was a meeting going on in the sky. The meeting concluded, but a name of a country was left written in the sky. As I looked, this nation's name was spelled out one letter at a time by a laser beam.

As I turned to look again, the horses turned out to be human beings, including women with babies strapped on their backs, the way some African women strap their babies. I counted sixteen persons as each turned to leave the meeting and then filed out as a jury would do after rendering their verdict.

Although I had this dream years ago, I still do not understand much of it. I am sure it is one of those dreams that its meaning will unfold as time goes on. But as I prepare to conclude this book, I now know to a certain degree that, among the people God is seeking to use to execute His judgement on nations, are many ordinary women like Jael, Heber's wife. (see Judges 4:21) He will also use nursing mothers or mothers with children strapped on their backs, together with widows who serve as the unsung army in the Body of Christ.

They will form a part of God's army:

To execute vengeance on the nations, and punishment on the peoples; to bind their kings with chains, and their nobles with fetters of iron; to execute on them the written judgement—this honour have all His saints. Praise the Lord! (Psalms 149:7-9)

The Lord further reminds us that we are mighty and must judge justly and show no partiality to the wicked. We must defend the poor, fatherless, needy, and afflicted.

God stands in the congregation of the mighty; He judges among the gods. How long will you judge unjustly, and show partiality to the wicked? Selah. Defend the poor and the fatherless; do justice to the afflicted and needy. Deliver the poor and needy; free them from the hand of the wicked. (Psalm 82:1-4)

"Selah" means to pause or think upon these things. If we but one moment pause and reflect on our position to do justly, we can hardly shut our eyes and allow the wicked to prevail in our society or pass by a needy person and not help. Isaiah reminds us that for: fasting to be heard by God, for the bonds of wickedness to be loosed, for heavy burdens to be undone, for the oppressed to go free and for every yoke to be broken, we must do the following:

> *Is it not to share your bread with the hungry, and that you bring to your house the poor who are cast out; when you see the naked, that you cover him, and not hide yourself from your own flesh?* (Isaiah 58:7)

This is not a "here today, gone tomorrow" program to support the needy. The good news is that the Church can now wake up to its responsibility.

We acknowledge that the process of healing and recovery takes time. It requires much wisdom and patience and quite often precision on the part of those standing alongside the bereaved and the hurting. But the challenge for the Church is to rise up and continue in our commitment to support and care for the widows, the fatherless, the orphans, and the poor in our midst.

While we acknowledge that the Church is actively engaged in orphanage projects, a similar support for widows will save a generation. As we say, "A widow empowered is a generation saved." By so doing, we are not only being like Christ, who is always moved by compassion, but we are also extending His Kingdom.

PRAYER:

Heavenly Father, everything about you is redemptive. As you redeem my situation, please interpret it to best suit the purpose it is designed for. Cause me to blossom, flourish and prosper in it, in Jesus Name.

Chapter ELEVEN
At The City Gates

I believe that there is something about a widow at the city gate that is connected to the role of the prophet with regard to a city.

I also believe that the prophet's ministry is the one role that functions in all five senses to effectively serve the Body of Christ. Therefore, an effective use of this office can bring God's Kingdom to a city.

This is not to say that a prophet should go seek out a widow in order to have a breakthrough in a city. This is simply a call to look a bit further into the prophetic role in connection with a widow. There is a resonance that prophets should have in their hearts when in contact with a widow, because, as seers, they can discern her situation in a deep sense that may not be obvious or even apparent to the other ministries in the Body of Christ.

A prophet will not only hear and see, but will carry out the instruction of the Lord, however unusual the command might be. For example, the prophet Elijah was sent to a widow in Zarephath who may well have died for lack of food. Regardless of what this might have done to Elijah's reputation, he carried out this command.

When Elijah was sent to the widow of Zarephath he met her at the city gate, and although nothing was said of revival breaking forth in the city, the Lord Jesus' reference to it suggests that the testimony of Elijah's visit to that city could not have gone unnoticed (see Luke 4:25-28)

The other widow mentioned with reference to a city gate, is the Widow of Nain, whose only son died and was raised by the Lord. (see Luke 7:11-17)

Both widows are identified by the cities they came from, and both are met at the city gate. It was easy for Elijah to spot the Zarephath widow at the entrance of the city, gathering sticks to cook her last meal for her and her son.

The Lord Jesus was entering the city of Nain with a crowd when he came upon the Widow of Nain.

These very sad situations are the ones which demanded attention without the widows having to ask for help. They had resigned themselves to their seemingly hopeless situations; they were willingly to accept their lot in life.

A prophetic engagement with a widow will not only transform the widow's life, but also like yeast in dough, it will spread throughout the community or city.

Provision and Blessing

I hope this is not overstated, but a careful study will reveal that this special group of people in the Body of Christ, the widows, is dear to the Father's heart. Their care should no longer be ignored or neglected.

Widows are mentioned constantly in the Bible through the Old Testament by prophets like Isaiah, Jeremiah, Ezekiel, Zephaniah, Zechariah, Malachi, and especially Elijah and Elisha. These stories have become favourites among pastors and ministers, as they are also so much more than just a call for the recognition of widows.

I believe that the lack of recognition of the role of prophets in many churches, compared to that of the rest of the five-fold ministries, has also led to a lack of recognition for the widows. I also believe that prophets should seek out widows and become voices for them, as did the Old Testament prophets and the patriarch, Job.

We don't read any accounts in the Bible where leaders rendered help to widows or where the widows were able to approach them in their time of need.

We understand from Scriptures (Deuteronomy 26: 12-15) that widows, orphans, strangers and the Levites should partake of tithes in the House, but we know that most local churches do not have funds in place for widows. I believe that a portion of a local church's tithe income must go to the support of widows, orphans and strangers in the church and not just for administrative costs

This is something the Lord Jesus made specific reference to — the injustice of widows being reduced to abject poverty by the leaders who 'devour widows' houses' and yet make long prayers. (see Mark 12:38-40)

As a result, there should be no reason why a widow is not able to approach her local pastor for financial help if the need arises, but we know that this was often not true in the Bible days, nor is it the case in our present day.

The widow whose sons were to be sold into slavery if her debt was not paid could not approach the leaders then, but instead went to Elisha, the prophet, for help. Even the widow at Zarephath received help from Elijah and not seek any support from the leaders of her city. You might say that Zarephath was a Gentile city, but I do not think it would have been any different in Israel either. One of the sins for which the Lord God rebuked Israel was their oppression of this silent and voiceless group, not defending the fatherless or pleading the cause of widows.

Hence, I believe that it is the place of the prophet to become a voice for this silent community living on the margins of society.

Another prophet that I would like to mention is King David. King David was a prophet, as we see from his Messianic Psalms. (see Psalm 22; 45; 110)

There is a very interesting account of King Saul's concubine, Rizpah, who was a widow. (see 2 Samuel 21:1-14) She petitioned to protect the bodies of King Saul's dead sons who had been lawfully killed following his broken covenant with the Gibeonites which brought about a three-year famine in Israel. Her campaign had brought her to the attention of King David. King David's response to Rizpah was to give King Saul and his house a proper burial thus bringing the three-year famine to an end.

The interesting thing about this account is that we can easily relate to this story and yet overlook that it is a widow whom the Lord uses to bring about the healing of the land. I have already mentioned many others, like Anna the prophetess, Tamar, the widow at Zarephath, the widow and her mite, and many more widows who are seldom preached about.

The place of widows and prophets and their significance in the Church should be awakened and recognised for good. This will lead to greater effectiveness in the expansion of God's Kingdom.

Releasing Revival

A few years ago, on November 22, 1999, the late Derek Prince came to Kensington Temple, the local church I attended while living in London. It has been the only church I've known since coming to the United Kingdom in April 1988. It is a very vibrant church, having over 110 nationalities in attendance by the time that he visited.

Pastor Prince was eighty-four years old when he visited our church and gave a message on widows, orphans, and the needy. He admitted that in all his over fifty-eight years of preaching, he had not heard a sermon on this topic, nor had it entered into his mind to teach on it, until the Lord drew his attention to it.

Derek Prince understood from Scripture that the nature of God is His heart for the widows and orphans. (see Psalm 68:5) The Law of Moses, the prophets, and the New Testament teachings are all full of the Church's responsibility towards this target group.

One thing that struck me very deeply was his declaration that recognition and carrying out our responsibilities to the whom the Lord uses to bring about the healing of the land. I have already mentioned many others, like Anna the prophetess, Tamar, the widow at Zarephath, the widow and her mite, and many more widows who are seldom preached about.

The place of widows and prophets and their significance in the Church should be awakened and recognised for good. This will lead to greater effectiveness in the expansion of God's Kingdom.

Releasing Revival

A few years ago, on November 22, 1999, the late Derek Prince came to Kensington Temple, the local church I attended while living in London. It has been the only church I've known since coming to the United Kingdom in April 1988. It is a very vibrant church, having over 110 nationalities in attendance by the time that he visited.

Pastor Prince was eighty-four years old when he visited our church and gave a message on widows, orphans, and the needy. He admitted that in all his over fifty-eight years of preaching, he had not heard a sermon on this topic, nor had it entered into his mind to teach on it, until the Lord drew his attention to it.

Derek Prince understood from Scripture that the nature of God is His heart for the widows and orphans. (see Psalm 68:5) The Law of Moses, the prophets, and the New Testament teachings are all full of the Church's responsibility towards this target group.

One thing that struck me very deeply was his declaration that recognition and carrying out our responsibilities to the widows, orphans, and the poor is a "key to releasing revival in Great Britain."

Two years later, I felt ready to carry out my passion for widows. I visited my spiritual mentors in Holland — Fritjof and Froyke Eibrink-Jansen — where my passion for widows had all begun. As Reverend Froyke prayed for me, she mentioned exactly what Derek Prince had said — our care for this group is a key to revival in the Body of Christ.

Besides my contacts in Amsterdam, I also approached a minister of the Gospel in London. While praying for me, she declared the very same thing. We know from Scripture that, at the mouths of two or three witnesses, a word is established.

Supposing I discountenanced my two mentors — how was I to ignore a well-respected, eighty-four year old teacher of the Word and author of so many Christian books, whose ministry has blessed so many worldwide?

In his sermon that evening, Derek Prince said that he believed that our care for widows, orphans, and the needy is a key to 'releasing revival' in the Church.

In the book *Dream Language: The Prophetic Power of Dreams, Revelations, and the Spirit of Wisdom* by James W. and Michal Ann Goll, (Shippensburg, PA: Destiny Image, 2006) he recalls a dream which he calls "A House That is Built to Last."

> I was at a construction site watching as a cement truck poured layer after layer of concrete into the foundation of a house. Two angels, symbolising the jealousy of God, stood at the two front corners of the foundation, overseeing the construction. ...As each layer of concrete set, words appeared in the foundation, similar to the handwriting on the wall recorded in the Book of Daniel.

At the right front corner of the first layer appeared the words, "Jesus Christ, the Messiah of the Jew and the Gentile." The left corner read, "Apostles and prophets; fathers and mothers of the church ages."

...As the second layer of concrete was poured, the word "Integrity" appeared on the right corner and the word 'Humility' on the left. ...Across the front of the third layer were the words: "Intimate worship from a pure heart." And, finally, the fourth layer of concrete bore the words, "God's heart for the poor and the desperate." Shooting out from those words was the phrase, "God's healing grace."

I make reference to this dream to show that the construction of the Lord's building is incomplete without the care for the needy and poor in the Body of Christ. As we engage in prayer for revival in the Church and in our cities and nations, I believe simple care for members of the Body that are invisible and in need of more attention, will bring speedy answers to our prayer. Paul puts it this way:

> *On the contrary, those parts of the body that seem to be weaker are indispensable, and the parts that we think that are less honourable we treat with special honour. And the parts that are un-presentable are treated with special modesty, while our presentable parts need no special treatment. But God has combined the members of the body and has given greater honour to the parts that lacked it, so that there should be no division in the body, but that its parts should have equal concern for each other. If one part suffers, every part suffers with it; if one part is honoured, every part rejoices with it* (1 Corinthians 12:22-26 NIV)

I believe that this silent community that we have unconsciously marginalised and even neglected, is the indispensable part of the Body of Christ that should be treated with special modesty. Rightfully so, when you consider that the Lord shows great honour to widows and orphans, as we have read throughout Scripture.

Not only do we realise that this is at the Lord's heart, but it is also a command from Him. We see how the Lord Jesus illustrated sacrificial giving and persistent prayer by narrating the accounts of two widows. We have extensively mentioned the account of the widow who gave her mite and the account of the persistent widow.

In the Sermon on the Mount, in Matthew, when teaching on the lifestyle of the Kingdom of God, the Lord Jesus magnifies the teachings on giving and prayer, among other things.

Using these two widows as examples of extreme giving and extreme praying, they provide a further example of going the extra mile, a characteristic of the Kingdom lifestyle.

The lifestyle of the Kingdom of God is one of living in the superlative and, consequently, in the supernatural. It is the ministry of,

> *Let your light so shine before men, that they may see your good works and glorify your Father in heaven.* (Matthew 5:16)

This is also seen in the bearing of much fruit:

> *By this My Father is glorified, that you bear much fruit; so you will be My disciples.* (John 15:8)

This the Lord's emphasis in teaching His Body the principle of going above and beyond the call of duty to express His Kingdom culture.

Widows in the lineage of our Lord Jesus

I have often wondered why the Bible recorded widows in the lineage of our Lord Jesus Christ. As I prayed and sought the Lord about this, I believe He gave me an answer one midnight as I waited on Him on this matter.

I felt the Lord began to speak to me about the pain of separation through death. The fall of man in Genesis brought spiritual death to humanity, which resulted in the whole of the human race being separated from God. As a result, God knew loss, grief, and separation right from the beginning when the human race died a spiritual death by eating the forbidden fruit.

Akin to this, but not in any way comparable to the Lord's, is the pain one feels at the death of a loved one, resulting in physical separation. As I pondered on this, it became obvious to me why God drafted widows into His divine plan of salvation for humankind. It takes one pain to recognise another, and our God is no exception, especially since He describes His relationship with the Church as that of a bridegroom and bride and His relationship with Israel as that of husband and wife.

Tamar, the first widow to be recorded in the Bible, became the mother of Zerah and Perez, from whose lineage includes Boaz, the husband of the widow Ruth.

Boaz, one of the best examples of a kinsman redeemer in the Old Testament, incorporated the Gentile race into the Messianic line by marrying the Moabitess, Ruth. This makes these two widows examples of God's heart for full redemption and restoration.

The picture of recovery after a loss — spiritual or physical death — is given here to show the plentiful redemption we have in God through Jesus Christ. The Bible tells us that "...for with the Lord there is... abundant redemption" (Psalm 130:7)

There are widows in Scripture who are not often mentioned, although not in the lineage of our Lord.

In 1 Kings there is the account of Huram. His mother was a widow from the tribe of Naphtali, and he was a highly skilled and experienced craftsman in all kinds of bronze work.

> *Now King Solomon sent and brought Huram from Tyre. He was the son of a widow from the tribe of Naphtali, and his father was a man of Tyre, a bronze worker; he was filled with wisdom and understanding, and skill in working with all kinds of bronze work. So he came to King Solomon and did all his work.* (1 Kings 7:13-14)

King Solomon assigned him to do the furnishing of the temple, and 1 Kings 7:40 tells us that Huram finished all the work he had undertaken for King Solomon in the temple of the Lord. This account truly justifies the saying, "A widow helped is a generation saved."

Another account of a widow's son is Jeroboam, whose mother was called Zeruah. (see 1 Kings 11:26) Jeroboam was a man of standing, and when King Solomon saw how well the man worked, he appointed him to be in charge of his entire labour force in the house of Joseph. He later on became the king of the ten northern tribes of Israel following the prophecy of Ahijah.

It is interesting to note that attention is drawn to these widows because of their sons' significant roles in building the temple of the Lord and the house of Israel.

A note to the Special Ladies

When Jesus therefore saw His mother, and the disciple whom he loved standing by, He said to His mother, "Woman, behold your son!" Then He said to the disciple, "Behold your mother!" And from that hour that disciple took her to his own home. (John 19:26-27)

When the Lord commended Mary to John, He also asked Mary to look after John. This invariably means that the Church is also the responsibility of the widow.

The widow has a responsibility to the Church, and the account of Anna, the prophetess, is a case in point. (see Luke 2:36-38) She, together with Simeon, prayed in the birth of our Lord Jesus Christ.

We know from Scripture that the Holy Spirit will move on men to pray when the fulfilment of a prophecy is drawing near. Daniel understood from reading the prophecies of Jeremiah, that the time to return from captivity in Babylon was at hand. Therefore, Daniel set himself to seek the Lord.

The widows, especially the ones who have passed the age of remarriage, owe the Church the duty of fasting and prayer. Needless to say, Anna was a young widow who chose not to remarry, but instead, gave herself to fasting and prayer day and night. The Lord remembered the labour of love she showed for the sake of the promise.

The parable of the persistent widow in Luke 18 highlights the place of persistent prayer by the Lord's saints in His Body, but more so for the widow. You can take care of the Lord's Body in a special way by bending your knees in prayer.

Although the Church is the Bride of Christ, God is the Husband to the widow.

> *Do not fear, for you will not be ashamed; neither be disgraced, for you will not be put to shame; for you will forget the shame of your youth, and will not remember the reproach of your widowhood any more. For your Maker is your husband, the Lord of Hosts is His name; and your Redeemer is the Holy One of Israel; He is called the God of the whole earth* (Isaiah 54:4-5)

Whether you had your loved one for ninety years, nine months or just nine days, and you cannot stop shedding tears Remember... We all came from the Maker, and if your loved one is with Him, then Heaven cannot be so far away.

PRAYER:

Heavenly Father, help to make me a co-labourer in prayer with our Lord Jesus Christ as you tug at my heart string for something you want to see done and accomplish on earth. May your Kingdom come and your will be done on earth as it is in heaven, in Jesus Name.

Chapter **TWELVE**

A Hurting Mother

As mothers, we often forget that children are God's gifts to us and that we are merely caretakers. We only have them for a short while, to influence them and impact them for the rest of their lives, and the baton goes on and on.

We have instructions in the Bible on how to raise our children, but what happens when a mother does all she knows how to do and a son or a daughter goes his or her own way like the prodigal son?

> *...A certain man had two sons. And the younger of them said to his father, "Father, give me the portion of goods that falls to me." So he divided to them his livelihood. And not many days after, the younger son gathered all together, journeyed to a far country, and there wasted his possessions with prodigal living. (Luke 15:11-13)*

Although, this is a story of a father and his sons, this story could also relate to a mother. The mother is left with an unimaginable pain for her child. There is the pain of not knowing if he will ever come back home or in what shape he will arrive at your door.

The thoughts of, "What could I have done differently?" and the sleepless nights, leave you helpless, making the pain worse. You have to face friends, neighbours, and even church folks, who constantly remind you of what seems to be a failure of your motherhood.

Casting this care on the Lord is the one and, in my opinion, only choice we have; because Scripture says, He cares for us. He will fix it for us.

About two years ago, a dear friend of mine suddenly lost contact with her first son, who lived in America. What seemed to be a silence of a week or two rolled into months, a year, and then two years. My friend was beside herself and we were too, as we began to call on the Lord for contact between them to resume.

As time wore on, I found it hard to ask after her son, expecting that soon we would hear from him and end this whole nightmare of not knowing if he was alive or dead or thrown in jail somewhere. My friend told me that sometimes she felt her head aching and her heart wrenching with the pain of not knowing how to go about looking for her son. But as she remembered that there were other saints carrying this pain with her, she consoled herself to take one day at a time.

One morning in March of this year, as I was doing my ironing, I felt a strong urge to pray for my friend's son. After praying briefly, I called my friend to encourage her that God was on the case as usual, and that hope was near. Within four weeks of this phone call, my friend came visiting with the news that she had finally heard from her son. How we worshipped the Lord for answers to prayers!

Conversely, there is a pain that a hurting woman goes through in marriage when she knows that she is unloved in the marriage relationship or unable to have babies. The grief that comes with that knowledge is very sad and frustrating and becomes expressed in day-to-day living. It carries with it the sense of loneliness and rejection and even inferiority.

Leah and Rachel were two sisters who faced these situations, and they leave us wondering whether one difficulty is better than the other.

Each situation has its pain and grief, but our ability to draw strength from God and trust that His grace will not leave us without comfort, brings us to a place of hopeful resignation. We know that we carry His Hope which does not make us ashamed. Leah finally came to this realisation when she had her fourth son, Judah, and called him "Praise."

> *And she conceived again and bore a son, and said, "Now I will praise the Lord." Therefore she called his name Judah. Then she stopped bearing.* (Genesis 29:35)

The God of All Comforts

Our consolation is always from the Lord and not from man, not even our own husband. The Lord saw that Leah was unloved and sought to fix it by opening her womb. Leah could not fix it, nor could her father who arranged the marriage. It took Leah a little while to know that the Lord had seen her affliction and had rewarded her with sons. She finally came to the place of thanksgiving and praise to the Lord.

On the other hand, Rachel was struggling with all kinds of emotions, including envy, and she even grew angry at Jacob. But at the appointed time, God listened to her and remembered her.

> *Then God remembered Rachel, and God listened to her and opened her womb. And she conceived and bore a son, and said, "God has taken away my reproach." So she called his name Joseph, and said, "The Lord shall add to me another son."* (Genesis 30:22-24)

When we remind ourselves that God listens and He remembers, we can easily lay down our grief and can start to become busy living a healthy emotional life by seeking ways to be a blessing to other people. Leah's rejection and Rachel's barrenness became journeys of faith that ultimately brought them both children of great destinies. From Levi, the priestly tribe arose that served the Lord and ministered over the entire nation of Israel, and from Judah was born King David and the royal lineage from which descended our Lord Jesus. Rachel gave birth to Joseph who was a vital person in the life and history of Israel.

God always has a plan and purpose for any circumstance or situation that we face, even if it is beyond our comprehension.

Responding to Pain

As we look at Hannah, the first woman whose prayer is recorded in the Bible, we see a woman who approached God with weeping and anguish of soul. Whether we are waiting on the Lord for the fruit of the womb or for a prodigal child to come home, our first point of call should be the Lord.

When a woman is hurting within herself in the manner of a consuming ache of inadequacy provoked by unkind words, she is forced to bring prayers with passion to God. Mere words will not do, as we see in the case of Hannah.

> *And it happened, as she continued praying before the Lord, that Eli watched her mouth. Now Hannah spoke in her heart; only her lips moved, but her voice was not heard. Therefore, Eli thought she was drunk. So Eli said to her, "How long will you be drunk? Put your wine away from you!" But Hannah answered and said, "No, my lord, I am a woman of sorrowful spirit. I have drunk neither wine nor intoxicating drink, but have poured out my soul before the Lord."* (1 Samuel 1:12-15)

A desperate situation will bring one to a place of reckless abandonment, but this should be wisely channelled to God in prayer as you reach a place where you can pour out your soul to God like Hannah did.

I found this case true with a young Christian widow whose young son lived in her home country. She received news of him roaming the streets with no food or shelter. She told me the pain she felt when she heard the news, and the shame she felt, as her son was no longer referred to by his name but by hers.

One day in September 2007, as she wept uncontrollably about the whole situation at the end of a conference, the visiting preacher drew her attention to the story of Hannah. She began to draw comfort from that story. Since then, she has not only heard from her son, but her son is happily settled with a member of her family, as she awaits their reunion.

Women are not known to give up easily, and this persistence, if used correctly, is a powerful tool to change any situation for the better. Hannah used what was available to her

— tears and passion — to seek God, until her change came.

I do believe that there are certain situations you cannot shift alone, and therefore the support of godly women should be the cushion you lean on. Whether it is faith for an unsaved husband or children who have left home, the Bible speaks of the prayer of agreement.

> *Again I say to you that if two of you agree on earth concerning anything that they ask, it will be done for them by My Father in heaven.* (Matthew 18:19)

As we go through such trying moments, our emotions undergo changes, as does our whole perspective on life. A maturity comes from that place of intimacy with the Lord, because you know you have touched His heart and that He has heard you.

Hannah went home knowing that God had heard her cry for a son, and Scripture records that her husband knew her and she conceived and gave birth to Samuel. Her magnificent praise of God at the birth of her son foreshadows that of Mary, the mother of our Lord Jesus, when she visited her cousin Elizabeth. (see 1 Sam. 2:1-10; Luke 1:46-55)

Whatever you have been through as a woman or a mother, the Lord will certainly bring you to a place where you can say like Hannah:

> *There is none holy as the Lord: for there is none beside thee: neither is there any rock like our God.* (1 Samuel 2:2 KJV)

The *kairos* moment in the history of humankind was taking place as our Lord Jesus hung on the Cross with the weight of the whole world on His shoulders, yet He remembered to put His mother in the care of John the beloved. He made sure that Mary, his mother, should have a complete care when he handed her to John.

The Bible does not say much about Joseph, His earthly father, after the Lord Jesus stayed behind in Jerusalem at the age of twelve. The Lord did not assume that James, Jude, and His sisters would look after Mary. Instead, He gave the Church a model of how to care for the vulnerable in our midst. In fact, He handed His mother to the Church to take care of, as John became one of the elders in the Church in Jerusalem as we later read in the Book of Acts.

If ever the Church is in doubt as to our responsibility to widows, the needy, and the vulnerable in our midst, this charge to John at the Cross should hopefully wake the Church up.

Earlier in the Book of Luke, when the Lord Jesus was presented to God at the temple, as it was written in the Law, Simeon prophesied to Mary: "(Yes, a sword will pierce through your own soul also), that the thoughts of many hearts may be revealed" (Luke 2:35)

I do not believe that even this prophecy could have prepared her for what she would have to watch her son endure n the Cross at the hands of evil men. From placing the new born Jesus in a manger, to watching each drop of His redeeming blood fall from the Cross, Mary understood the God-given intimacy that only a mother can share with her child. Yet I am not persuaded that any mother could comprehend the pain Mary went through as she stood there and watched the unimaginable happen to her Son. Truly, as prophesied by Simeon, a sword went through her soul.

Mary responded to this pain by placing her entire life on the altar of God's purpose and plan when she said to the angel Gabriel,

> *"Behold the maidservant of the Lord! Let it be to me according to your word." (Luke 1:38)*

Following that, at the visit to her cousin Elizabeth, Mary greatly magnified the Lord by the Holy Spirit.

Mary's prophetic song, which in many ways is similar to Hannah's after the birth of Samuel, is her praise song to God for regarding and helping the lowly and the poor. (see 1 Sam. 2:8) Even before Mary saw the manifestation of the Lord Jesus' ministry, she knew by the Spirit that God's heart was to raise the lowly.

Uprooting Bitterness

There is a story I feel stirred to mention here, and Kathryn (not her real name) is happy for me to share it.

This young lady lost her husband to AIDS and obviously had contracted the disease herself through him. When her situation came to light, she was given only a few hours to live by the doctors. When she miraculously survived those hours, she was observed for a week or more, and then sent home. She was discharged with a prognosis of two years to live, maximum.

It is now way past two years since the doctor's prognosis and she is still alive. But there was pain she was carrying that she found hard to shift — the anger towards her late husband for giving her this deadly disease that appears to have no cure. She felt that at least her husband was dead and gone, but she was left to struggle with this disease alone, fearing what the bleak future held.

However, as she began to bring this pain to the Lord, the story of the widow's oil in 2 Kings came to her mind.

> *A certain woman of the wives of the sons of the prophets cried out to Elisha, saying, "Your servant my husband is dead, and you know that your servant feared the Lord. And the creditor is coming to take my two sons to be his slaves.* (2 Kings 4:1)

Although the husband of this widow had left her with debt that could have resulted in her sons being sold into slavery, the widow knew where to go for help and did not sulk in her situation.

Kathryn, too, now knows that it is no use to hold a grudge against her late husband, but to trust God to remedy the situation for her like He did for the widow with the oil. She has also found the support of her local fellowship very helpful; there are people walking with her through the valley of the shadow of death.

As she shares her testimony of how God raised her from her potential deathbed when she hardly knew the Lord, she knows that her condition will not result in death but bring glory to God. She is now able to go past the hurt and pain and anger against her late husband and is happily studying and planning for her future with hope.

At any given time, many of God's saints are suffering some kind of financial debt, broken relationship, or a physical ailment. Yet the Lord weeps with those who weep and rejoices with those who are rejoicing. A huge problem in the church is when Christians look at brothers and sisters in constraint and assume that they are less favoured by God.

Our position should be to raise our shield and stand side by side with our brother while the storms of life blow over. It may just be that the person is going through circumstance that make him a current witness, or God may be preparing the individual for future usefulness and fruitfulness. The power of solidarity in suffering will enable the saint to respond to pain easily and overcome it quickly. It is said, "A problem shared is a problem solved." An example of solidarity in suffering is drawn from Hebrews.

Remember the prisoners as if chained with them—those who are mistreated—since you yourselves are in the body also. (Hebrews 13:3)

We know that the topic under discussion here is not literal prison, but the situations and circumstances that hold us down. Contrary to what Cain thought, we are our brother's and our sister's keepers.

Our response to pain, loss of any kind, disappointments and betrayals can become His appointments to shape us into men and women of destiny. A goldsmith will allow gold to stay in the fire until he can see his reflection in it. So too, our heavenly Father refines our faith that is purer than gold to reflect His image. He uses every pain and each trouble to 'purify' us until we represent a picture of Him.

A huge step to overcoming pain of any kind is to avoid a seed of resentment which allows bitterness to take root.

Looking carefully lest anyone fall short of the grace of God, lest any root of bitterness springing up cause trouble, and by this many become defiled. (Hebrews 12:15)

The writer of Hebrews draws upon Moses' instruction to the children of Israel in Deuteronomy:

> *So that there may not be among you man or woman of family or tribe, whose heart turns away today from the Lord our God, to go and serve the gods of these nations, and that there may not be among you a root bearing bitterness or wormwood.* (Deuteronomy 29:18)

There is a choice to get better or get bitter at the circumstance and looking for someone to pin the blame on. In the case of death, we often not only blame the dead, but we blame God. The result is that we turn away from Him to the gods of self-pity, entertainment, alcohol, and even drugs.

We become what we look upon or meditate upon, and we remain a victim and not a victor. On the other hand, when we root out any seed of resentment like weeds from a garden, and replace them with God's grace, we clothe ourselves with His graciousness and goodness.

PRAYER:

Heavenly Father, thank you for the hope and relief your Spirit of comfort gives. Teach me to rely solely on the comfort of the Holy Spirit, knowing that He will make happen in my life, the promise of - 'Blessed are those who mourn, for they shall be comforted.' I thank you for your Word which is a guarantee, in Jesus Name.

Chapter THIRTEEN
Shedding The Past

It is easy to live with regret if one chooses to blame a circumstance or a person. Some people are never able to look back, but most of us keep looking back. This keeps us wondering what life would have been like had we done things differently. Those kinds of thoughts are what bind us up and keep us preoccupied with the past, eventually crippling us.

Seven years ago, I compiled a very small collection of thoughts entitled "Dear Vessel unto Honour," and one of them is:

Holding on to experiences that you should let go

Can put you on hold.

Permit not your mind

To rewind experiences that bind.

This and many other thoughts became my first baby steps to recovery from the loss of our stillborn baby, Ruth.

I learned that there are treasures in my trials. We all suffer loss through death, broken relationships, financial ruin and many other issues that often result in losing something or someone dear to us. Although pain and grief are part of life, if we do not give ourselves time to mourn and grieve, our wounds may never be cleaned and healed. But there is a time-span on mourning and grieving, as we find in God's rebuke to Samuel for his extended grief over the loss of Saul as king over Israel.

Samuel had extended his grief over Saul beyond the season God had appointed:

> *Now the Lord said to Samuel, "How long will you mourn for Saul seeing I have rejected him from reigning over Israel? Fill your horn with oil, and go; I am sending you to Jesse the Bethlehemite. For I have provided Myself a king among his sons."*
> (1 Samuel 16:1)

The transition from a season of grief to a fresh season is made by shedding the past. Be ready to move on when you feel the nudge of the Holy Spirit saying to you that you have stayed on this mountain too long (see Deuteronomy 1:6)

To access your new wine or oil, you must forget your yesterday. If Samuel had remained in the place of his grief over Saul, he would have missed his next assignment and the privilege of anointing, not just a king over Israel, but a man after God's own heart. Samuel was led to a man who respected and recognised his office as a prophet of God, who did not take matters into his own hands as Saul did.

Ecclesiastes tells us there is,

A time to weep, and a time to laugh; a time to mourn, and a time to dance. (see Eccles. 3:4)

You have wept and have mourned, but now is the time to lay down the grief clothes and take up singing, laughing and dancing. It is now a season of beauty for ashes, the oil of joy for mourning and the garment of praise for the spirit of heaviness.

Shedding the past involves putting away harsh words and complaints against God and beginning to fear His name. Then the Son of Righteousness will arise with healing in His wings.

As you begin to shed the past, the Son of Righteousness comes with healing for you, and you are therefore positioned to go forth, full of His anointing. By the reason of fatness, the yoke of the past is broken. Your path begins to shine brighter and brighter:

But the path of the just is as the shining light, that shines more and more unto the perfect day. (Proverbs 4:18 KJV)

Progress requires that we emerge and come out of the old, becoming a new person in a new place. God's commitment to you allows Him to carry you through any circumstance if you let Him. After all, He will not only bring you out of the miry clay and set your feet on a rock; He will put a new song, yes, a new song in your mouth. People will begin to see it and fear and put their trust in the Lord. (see Psalm. 40:2-3)

The New Season

Today, as we look at the winter seasons of our lives that we are going through and have been through, one thing is sure

— we must embrace our new season of life and go forth in it if we do not want to get stuck in the past.

Spiritual growth often thrives in the bed of adversities.

Every fresh season often comes with a new identity, and it becomes the person to wear it well with the grace that the Lord supplies. Some of the old identities we have carried in the past are those of bereavement, shame, abandonment, rejection, failure, depression and the list goes on. However, as we come into a new season, we are set free from the captivity of the past as we identify with our new season and new assignment.

For example, when Joshua came into a new season of his life, Moses gave him a new name:

> *These are the names of the men whom Moses sent to spy out the land. And Moses called Hoshea the son of Nun, Joshua.* (Numbers 13:16)

Similarly, Peter and Paul received new names as they were both coming into new assignments for their lives. Simon came into the revelation that Jesus Christ was the son of the Living God: "...You are the Christ, the Son of the living God" (Matt. 16:16)

At that point, he came upon a new name and a new identity with a new assignment.

> *And I [Jesus] also say to you that you are Peter, and on this rock I will build my church, and the gates of Hades shall not prevail against it. And I will give you the keys of the kingdom of heaven, and whatever you bind on earth will be bound in heaven, and whatever you loose on earth will be loosed in heaven.* (Matthew 16:18-19)

Peter moved from being a shaky reed to a firm rock of revelation, on whose confession the Church was built and by which it advanced.

Likewise, Saul became Paul when he had a life-changing encounter with the Lord on the road to Damascus. In fact, he was not known as Paul until Acts 13, following the meeting in which the prophets and teachers gathered together to minister to the Lord through fasting, and the Holy Spirit separated Paul and Barnabas for the work He had called them to.

Embracing our new season always comes with new identity. Whether it is coming away from a season of pain, bereavement, or violence, as it was with Paul, we can reach one of hope again. We can share the comfort of the Holy Spirit which we have received.

The new season requires a transition into a new place or office to be assumed. The challenge is to function in the new. Otherwise, the past season will interfere with the present, and we will be torn between the old and the new. Our Lord Jesus puts it this way:

> *No one puts a piece of unshrunk cloth on an old garment; for the patch pulls away from the garment, and the tear is made worse. Nor do they put new wine into old wineskins, or else the wineskins break, the wine is spilled, and the wineskins are ruined. But they put new wine into new wineskins, and both are preserved.*
> (Matthew 9:16-17)

Esther's account is a beautiful story of transition from a season of being an orphan to becoming a queen in the land where she had been taken as a captive, together with other Israelites. Esther responded to this new season without questions or negotiations and graciously accepted all the guidance and preparation she needed to function in her new role as a queen. She ultimately accomplished God's purpose and destiny for her life

Guidance and spiritual preparation are necessary for the new season of our lives so that we do not function in our new place with our old mentality.

> *And Mordecai had brought up Hadassah, that is, Esther, his uncle's daughter, for she had neither father nor mother. The young woman was lovely and beautiful. When her father and mother died, Mordecai took her as his own daughter. So it was, when the king's command and decree were heard, and when many young women were gathered at Shushan the citadel, under the custody of Hegai, that Esther also was taken to the king's palace, into the care of Hegai the custodian of the women. Now the young woman pleased him, and she obtained his favour; so he readily gave beauty preparations to her, besides her allowance. Then seven choice maidservants were provided for her from the king's palace, and he moved her and her maidservants to the best place in the house of the women.* (Esther 2:7-9)

Here was an unknown orphan who knew when to answer the call to a new status in life. Life is full of changes and shifting seasons. There are no permanent conditions or situations unless we choose to make them so.

Ruth, whom we have mentioned over and over in this book, was another young lady who knew when to shed her widowhood under the wisdom and guidance of Naomi. Through the transition of gleaning in the fields in a strange land, she embraced the new culture and people and went on to become a wife and a mother.

So Boaz took Ruth and she became his wife; and when he went in to her, the Lord gave her conception, and she bore a son. (Ruth 4:13)

Like Ruth, you have been through your winter season of bereavement, widowhood, migration to a foreign land, separation from loved ones, poverty, and menial jobs. Know that spring is here. It has come as it did for Ruth, for Esther, for Joseph, and for many more in the Bible.

In Sue Mayfield's book, *Living with Bereavement* (Oxford, England: Lion Hudson Place, 2008), she quotes Tom Gordon, chaplain at an Edinburgh Hospice.

He has his own version of Ecclesiastes 3:1-8 of the Bible passage titled: "The Season of Grief."

Every stage of grief has its season. And every facet of loss has its time.

A time for disbelief, and a time for harsh reality,

A time to know, and a time to be consumed by unknowing,

A time for clarity, and a time for uncertainty,

A time for public smiles, and a time for private tears,

A time to be thankful, and a time of regret,

A time of giving up, and a time for going on,

A time for living half a life, and a time of wanting to live again,

A time of then, and a time of now,

A time to feel hopeless, and a time to be positive,

A time of looking forward, and a time of wanting life to end,

A time of faith, and a time of doubt,

A time for holding on, and a time for letting go,

A time when steps are light, and a time when limbs are tired,

A time of hazy memories, and a time of instant recall,

A time for living with death, and a time for living with life,

A time of fruitfulness, and a time of growth,

A time of despair, and a time of purpose,

A time of emptiness, and a time of hope,

A time of rage, and a time for peace.

In all of these, the Lord Jesus whispers peace — His legacy to us in the midst of our troubled world.

> *...that in Me you may have peace. In the world you will have tribulation; but be of good cheer, I have overcome the world.* (John 16:33)

PRAYER:

Heavenly Father, I choose to bask in your sun, as Your Sun of Righteousness rises on me with healing in His wings. I yield to your cure, remedy, medicine and restoration of health for my spirit, soul and body. Father, may your love repair any damage that grief and loss and its trauma had caused in my soul and life and bring me to a tranquil state of mind as I enter my new season of hope and purpose, in Jesus Name.

Conclusion

As I conclude this book, I draw your attention again to the story of the Good Samaritan. The theme of this story is that of showing compassion to anyone who is hurting.

As we seek to bring care and compassion back into the Church and our communities, we are simply going back to our first love for Jesus Christ. This love moved us to tell someone about the Good News of the Love of God, and it moved us to show God's kindness wherever we went.

We went about doing good, not only to a neighbour who was far away in another country, but also to one who was next door and on the next street. We knew when a brother or sister in the church needed a cooking pan or a lawn mower. Yes, the ministry of care amidst our many programs is coming back to the Body of Christ!

The lawyer who stood up to test Jesus asked, "Who is my neighbour?"

> *And behold, a certain lawyer stood up and tested Him, saying, "Teacher, what shall I do to inherit eternal life?" He said to him, "What is written in the law? What is your reading of it?" So he answered and said, "You shall love the Lord your God with all your heart, with all your soul, with all your strength, and with all your mind,' and 'your neighbour as yourself." And He said to him, "You have answered rightly; do this and you will live." But he, wanting to justify himself, said to Jesus, "And who is my neighbour?"*
>
> *Then Jesus answered and said, "A certain man went down from Jerusalem to Jericho, and fell among thieves, who stripped him of his clothing, wounded*

> him, and departed, leaving him half dead. Now by chance a certain priest came down that road. And when he saw him, he passed by on the other side.
>
> ... But a certain Samaritan, as he journeyed, came where he was. And when he saw him, he had compassion. So he went to him and bandaged his wounds, pouring on oil and wine; and he set him on his own animal, brought him to an inn, and took care of him.
>
> ...So which of these three do you think was a neighbour to him who fell among thieves?" (Luke 10:25-31,33-34,36)

There is one thief, and his assignment is to steal, kill, and destroy anyone. (see John 10:10) That anyone is our neighbour who may have fallen into a situation, like the loss of a husband, a child, a relative, a job, a home or a church through betrayal, church politics, marriage breakup, estrangement, and you can name the rest. But Jesus came to give life and gave it in abundance. (see John 10:10)

We bear His life; we distribute it wherever we go to anyone who needs it, especially those in the household of faith.

> Therefore, as we have opportunity, let us do good to all, especially to those who are of the household of faith. (Galatians 6:10)

Our mission is to do good to all people, whether that means taking the Gospel to the utmost part of the world or standing with the hurting, visiting the orphans and widows in their time of affliction, or just holding out our hand in loving comfort to touch and help somebody.

It is a Kingdom of doing justly, loving to show mercy, and walking humbly with our God. (see Micah 6:8)

And we are partakers of this Kingdom.

For the Kingdom is His

The power and the glory

Forever and ever

Amen

A Prayer Inviting Jesus into Your Heart

Father, I come to you acknowledging that Jesus Christ died on the cross to take my place so I can be accepted by You in Him.

I confess and repent of my sins and make a choice today to ask Him into my heart as my Lord and Saviour. By your Spirit, I receive the grace to follow and be Your disciple all the days of my life.

I thank You for washing me in His blood, choosing to love, receive and accept me as your adopted child, in Jesus Name.

Amen.

About The Author

Some years ago, the passion to reach and give recognition to widows and orphans with focus on widows, reached a point in her heart that she gathered a few Christian friends to pray and seek directions from the Lord.

Helen Aigbe-Joseph discovered that the support and recognition that the early Church gave to widows within the Body of Christ seemed to be lacking in our present-day Church. Responding to this passion, she now seeks and works with pastors and encourages support for widows, especially in their time of grief.

Helen believes in Kingdom reconciliation, relationship, and restoration in the believer's walk with the Lord and community transformation through prayers. Overcoming, and not coping, is the key to victorious Christian living.

Helen is married to Reverend Kingsley and they have three daughters, Stephanie, Salome and Daisy.

She travels and preaches locally and internationally in response to invitation.

info@vesselsofcompassion.org/

uviaj@hotmail.com

www.ingramcontent.com/pod-product-compliance
Lightning Source LLC
Chambersburg PA
CBHW070108120526
44588CB00032B/1388